A LIFE O

PRINCIPLES FOR A LIFE OF FAITH

A Manuel for discipleship

"For I am not ashamed of the Good News about Christ. It is the power of God at work, saving everyone who believes - This Good News tells us how God makes us right in his sight. This is accomplished from start to finish by faith"
"The just shall live by faith."
Romans 1:16,17

Roland Pletts

Cover photo by Author – "We Shall be Caught up"
This photo illustrates what faith is. For this man it is trusting entirely in the power of the helicopter and the skills of the pilot. In the same way, we are to put our faith entirely in the Lord.

This book can be ordered from www.lulu.com

ISBN 978 – 1 – 716 – 41205 - 9

Copyright reserved

Contents

Chapter 1 - **THY KINGDOM COME**
How to See the Kingdom, Enter the Kingdom and Live in the Kingdom – page 6.

Chapter 2 - **TWO KINGDOMS** – one of light, one of darkness, The Judgment of Satan - page 15.

Chapter 3 - **GOD'S KINGDOM THROUGH THE AGES**
The Fall of Mankind, God's Law, God's Grace, God's Plan for Believers – page 18.

Chapter 4 - **THE LAWS OF GOD'S KINGDOM**
God is Holy, Christ is our Mediator, The Royal Law – page 31.

Chapter 5 - **PRINCIPLES FOR LIFE IN CHRIST**
Repentance, Faith, Baptism, Service, Resurrection, Judgment, Eternal Life – page 40.

Chapter 6 - **TWO KINGDOMS AT WAR**
The Battle in the Hearts of People, Living a New Life, The Armour of God – page 58.

Chapter 7 – **PITFALLS TO A LIFE OF FAITH**
Confession, Sowing good seed – page 76.

Chapter 8 – **KEYS TO GROWING IN CHRIST**
Bible reading, Prayer, Spiritual Gifts – page 82.

Chapter 9 – **PROMISES FOR OUR FUTURE**
Heaven is our Home, The Key to a life of Faith – page 95.

REFERENCE NOTES - page 98

Introduction – God's Kingdom

The history of mankind is a long tale of sin and suffering but the Bible foretells that an age of peace and righteousness will come, in which "the lion will lie down with the lamb" and there will be universal harmony for mankind and nature. (Isaiah 11:6-9). All creation will be at peace. Many earthly kingdoms have come and gone with many attempts to bring peace but man's knowledge and power is unable to achieve lasting results: both scientists and emperors have failed. We are living at a time of global crisis. Only one person can fulfill this Biblical prediction, the man who died, rose again and inaugurated an eternal Kingdom, Jesus Christ, the Son of God. He overcame death and, he alone, has the power to establish God's Kingdom for he is the King of it. To enter it one must have faith in him. He is the Lion of Judah, who died as the "Lamb of God" and will reign forever on the throne of God. (Rev. 5:5,6). He is the "Prince of Peace". (Isaiah 9:6,7).

Various religions and cults claim they will establish a "New Age" but all have failed. It cannot come through religion, philosophy or science. The "good news" that Jesus proclaimed is about receiving the Kingdom of God. It is not about going to church. It is not anything that can be done by human wisdom or power. No scientists, generals, emperors, political leaders, prophets, apostles or apostolic church movements can establish the Kingdom despite what they may claim. Jesus came to reveal it and, when he returns, he will fully establish it. Only he, the Prince of Peace, is able to do so.

Many people think the Bible is obsolete but it is more up to date than tomorrow's newspaper and declares the only way of salvation. The Gospel is the truth that opens heaven. Because its message has been obscured by traditions and misinterpreted by cults, many people who consider themselves Christians have no grasp of the basic teachings of Christ or why he died on a cross. Many churchgoers are fed on liturgy, traditions, entertainment, anecdotes, and a whole lot more other than Biblical truth which leads to a personal faith in Christ. There has been an enormous increase in dubious and totally false "new age" concepts and practices which have crept into churches. The apostle Paul expressly instructed his young convert Timothy to "preach the Word" and nothing else. He also instructed Timothy to hold to the truth, for a time will come when many false teachers will "tickle" the ears of those who turn from sound doctrine to fables. (2 Tim. 3:13-17, 4:1-4). "New age" teaching, which exalts man not God, is now in many pulpits and has changed many Gospel truths. Believers in Christ must be grounded in "the faith". New converts need nurturing, as Hebrews 5:12-6:3 indicates. Followers of Jesus are not called to be passive churchgoers but active life disciples. Jesus called people to follow him and be discipled. He said he would give the keys of his Kingdom to those who obey him. (Matthew 16:18,19). These keys are so authoritative that they open or close Heaven itself. The apostle Peter was not given personal authority to open or close heaven but, based on the truth of the statement he made about Christ, he and believers after him were given the responsibility to declare the Gospel, which opens heaven to all who believe. It is by declaring, believing and receiving the true Gospel that the destiny of people and even nations is decided.

This presentation is about the Gospel of the Kingdom of God and considers how it comes to individuals and one day to the whole earth. Jesus taught us to pray; *"Thy Kingdom come, Thy will be done, on earth as it is in heaven".* He came to earth to seek the lost and by his death and resurrection he made eternal life available to those who want it. One day he will return and establish his Kingdom and those who receive him as Lord will enter it. This Kingdom is not just in the future; it exists even now and at his return will grow in power and glory until it controls all things. This is an absolute certainty. (Daniel 2:44). It will fill the whole earth, all mankind will come under its authority, and every knee will bow before Jesus. (Isa. 60:12, 45:23, Ps. 2:27-29, Rom. 14:11, Phil. 2:10). It is indestructible and survives the temporary rise and fall of all earthly kingdoms. King Jesus offers it to all who want to be part of it. (Matt. 22:34). You can become a citizen of his Kingdom by doing something very simple: repent and believe.

Do not be misled; only Jesus can give you that Kingdom and only he can establish it. If you want to be included in it you must surrender your life to him now. You must make him your King.

CHAPTER 1 - "THY KINGDOM COME"

Jesus commenced his public teaching with the announcement – "The Kingdom of God is at hand". (Mark 1:15). It was immediately apparent that the great theme of his teaching was the Kingdom of God. The Christian message is often loosely referred to as the Gospel, which actually means the **"Good News"**. It is about the Kingdom of Heaven, which is a real Kingdom with a King and a throne, a vast army, many citizens, and unlimited power.

Jesus said, **"Repent, for the Kingdom of God is at hand"**. He had a dynamic message and this was the way he introduced it. We should repent because God is making a tremendous offer, an invitation to be part of his Kingdom. Jesus was sent from heaven with terms for that Kingdom. When Jesus came, heaven invaded earth, and when he returns, he will fully establish his Kingdom.

Jesus said, **"This Gospel of the Kingdom shall be preached as a witness to all nations"**. (Mk. 13:10, LK. 24:47). It is therefore essential that we have a clear concept of what is meant by the Kingdom of God. The Gospel of God's Kingdom emphasises God's sovereign right to rule over all things. It exalts and magnifies God, recognising him as the King of the Universe, and declares his authority to rule everything, everywhere. It is our invitation to be part of it.

Jesus said, **"My Kingdom is not of this world"**. (John 18:36). In other words, it was not to be confused with, compared to, or linked with anything we might know on earth. It is not a mere kingdom. God's Kingdom is vast and universal, it is infinite and eternal – it includes everything – distant galaxies, indeed everything that exists. It will never end. (Isaiah 9:6,7). When Jesus came to earth, he announced the arrival of this Kingdom in a way not previously known. Christ came to deliver us from the kingdom of darkness. There are two kingdoms in opposition and conflict with one another. The present age is one of evil and because of sin darkness has engulfed the world. Christ came to break the power of sin and establish God's rule. The King of Heaven came disguised as a common carpenter. He conquered sin on the cross and died, rose from the dead, then ascended back to heaven and sat down on the highest throne of the universe. He reigns now and has all authority and power. However, his glory is veiled and many people simply do not believe it. Many people do not acknowledge his Lordship and even deny his existence. Yet God's Kingdom has always existed and is a reality today. The problem is that many people deny it and are covertly, or even overtly, hostile to it. They are blinded to it.

TO "SEE" THE KINGDOM – John 3:3-8.

<u>Jesus said</u>, "***no one can see the kingdom of God unless he is born again***". One night an educated and learned man called Nicodemus came to Jesus to find out what he taught. (John 3:1-36). Jesus came right to the point, and told Nicodemus that he needed divine help to see and understand God's Kingdom, and to enter it he needed to be "<u>born from above</u>". God's Kingdom is not a natural earthly kingdom but a spiritual Kingdom from heaven. It is unlike anything on earth and cannot be understood by natural means. The Holy Spirit must reveal it as it cannot be comprehended with the natural mind. The kingdoms of this world are subject to change and decay and are temporal. God's Kingdom is everlasting and has splendour beyond all earthly comparison. We read about great kingdoms of history such as those of Rome and Greece and we can visit their ruins but God's Kingdom has no ruins and will last forever.

<u>Jesus said</u>, "***There are some standing here who shall not taste of death till they see the Son of Man coming in His Kingdom***". (Matt. 16:28). Each time Jesus healed a person the Kingdom of God came to that person in a personal way. Every time Jesus raised the dead or did a miracle, he brought the future Kingdom into the present and made it real. People experienced it in their lives and, when they believed and received him as Lord, they "saw" the Kingdom. The same Kingdom is here today, right here for you to enter by believing and receiving Jesus as Lord and Saviour. It is governed by the commands of Christ alone who is its King. Its challenge confronts you. You are face to face with God's invitation to become a citizen of his eternal Kingdom. This is why Jesus said repent, make way for his Kingdom in your heart. No

man can serve two masters, there is no dual citizenship. If you have not surrendered your life to Jesus then he is not yet your King and his Kingdom is not ruling in you. God rules the entire universe and is offering you his eternal Kingdom which is where love, peace and righteousness reign. You can be part of it by receiving Jesus as your Lord and King. (Mark 12:34).

Jesus is the Son of God. The Bible reveals the eternal "Godhead" as the everlasting Father, the incorruptible Son, and the divine Holy Spirit. (Col. 2:9, Romans 1:20). This is declared in many scriptures. (John 14, 1 John 1, 2 John). Jesus was sent by the Father, was anointed by the Holy Spirit and was himself the eternal immortal Son. (Hebrews 1:5-13). He is totally one with God. (John 1:1 ff).

TO ENTER HIS KINGDOM, YOU MUST BE REBORN

God seeks for men and women to be part of his Kingdom, but to do so they must submit to Jesus as King. There is a "fallen nature" within every person which causes sin. It is universal and all mankind is under its shadow of death. Christ came to save the lost and when we put our faith in God, repent and believe in Jesus Christ, we are given the gift to become God's child. (Matt.18:11). We will be "born again" by God's Spirit. Jesus talked with Nicodemus and helped him to have faith to understand this. He told Nicodemus that he had to be born from above by God's Spirit and explained it as a spiritual rebirth. (John 1:12, 3:16,17). The apostle Peter spoke of it too. (1 Pet. 1:23).

There are many people who have some kind of belief in God but are not born by his Spirit. To experience this rebirth, we have to accept God's Son in an individual manner with a personal decision on our part. We become his children when we receive *his* Spirit through his Son. We thereby receive the "Spirit of adoption". (Rom. 8:15, Eph. 1:5, Gal. 4:5,6). God created all mankind but relates as Father only to those who are born as his children. We are all sinners and sin cannot enter the Kingdom of God. However, all who repent and receive Jesus as Lord are welcome, and by doing so we are born into his family. Jesus said this is the only way to enter his Kingdom. Those not willing to repent cannot enter for nothing impure gets in. Repentance is the only way in. It is impossible for people to enter unless they repent.

When Jesus died on the cross, he opened the way into the Kingdom of God. He became the gateway for forgiveness and acceptance. On each side of Jesus hung a thief and they represented the two ways of humanity. The one ends in loss and death, the other in Paradise. At the very doors of death one of the sinners entered God's Kingdom. What a miracle! Right then at the closing moments of his earthly life he received God's grace and mercy, was redeemed, forgiven and entered into the Kingdom. How did he do it? He cried out to the King of that Kingdom and said *"Lord, remember me when you come into your Kingdom."* As he watched Jesus suffering, he at first mocked him. However, he had a "change of mind" and believed. (Matt. 27:44, Luke 23:40-43). This is repentance - a "change of mind".

Jesus came to redeem the souls of men and women; this was the reason why he suffered on the cross. By dying he paid the price, with his blood, for the salvation of sinners. His death was foretold long ago in precise detail. (Isaiah 53). Jesus came into the world to save sinners (1 Tim. 1:15, Rom. 5:8-11, John 3:16,17). He did what no other person could do and that was to pay our penalty for sin and having suffered and died he came back to life so that through him we could have eternal life. The Bible says ***"Whosoever shall call upon the name of the Lord shall be saved"***. (Joel 2:32, Rom. 10:8-13).

Only Jesus can offer salvation and open God's Kingdom. He is the King and if you want to be part of his kingdom you must personally, by faith and deliberate purpose, receive him as Lord. When you crown him as Lord and receive him in your heart, his Spirit comes in and he lives within you, and he brings with him the reality and potential of his kingdom. When you receive Jesus then all of his kingdom and glory is included. One day God's kingdom will rule over all things but if you want to part of it, you must first receive him into your heart. Repentance and confession are the keys that open the way for forgiveness, and everything else God wants you to have.

His Kingdom does not come outwardly but inwardly. (Luke 17:20,21). When Jesus came, he was not welcomed with fanfare and trumpets, royal robes and worldly splendour. He was received only by those who gave him their hearts. There is no other way to enter the Kingdom apart from yielding our lives to him. It is not based upon religion, philosophy, ritual or ceremony. It does not come by baptism, confirmation, or any self-effort. It comes by receiving him as Lord in the simplicity of child-like faith and trust. Jesus said, *"I tell you the truth. Anyone who will not receive the Kingdom of God like a little child will not enter it."* We need to receive Christ as a child receives a gift. By doing this the gift of God becomes a reality in the life of individuals. God gives us salvation through his Son.

First and foremost, God's Kingdom comes into the *hearts* of men and women. The Bible describes his Kingdom as one of righteousness, peace, and joy in the Holy Spirit. These are things that mankind is desperately needing and unable to attain and that only God can give. Peace is elusive. Once Christ the "Prince of Peace" was crucified, war on this planet was inevitable. There can be no peace in the hearts of men or on earth until the Prince of Peace rules supreme. Christ alone brings peace to the sin-tossed hearts of men and women. People desperately search for happiness and yet reject the fountain and source of all lasting joy – God himself. It is the Holy Spirit who provides these things through a spiritual rebirth in which God creates a completely new person. (2 Cor. 5:17). By his Spirit he breathes his own nature into us and enables us to live life in his Kingdom. We have a foretaste of heaven on earth. We are delivered from sin to live as a child of God and a citizen of Heaven. One day God will establish his Kingdom on earth but we can personally experience it now.

YOU CAN LIVE IN HIS KINGDOM NOW

<u>Jesus said</u> **"Seek ye first the Kingdom of God and His righteousness and all these things will be added to you."** (Matt. 6:33).

Our part is to seek it: his part is to give it. If you have received him as King then he intends for you to live in his Kingdom. He makes it available now, not in some far-off place but right here. Christ invites you to enter and live in his Kingdom right now and to make it a reality in your life. You are saved to become a citizen of his Kingdom and to live in it, and experience its spiritual benefits and promises, and to serve Jesus as Lord. Who has ever heard of a kingdom without people who dedicate their lives to it? You continue to live on earth, contributing to society and serving him in a dark world. This does not mean you will not have difficulties, tests and trials.

Followers of Jesus are involved in a spiritual battle against temptation and spiritual powers. This is not a flesh and blood war but a spiritual conflict. There will be battles to fight but God has promised to be with us. When Christ is Lord we can live daily in his presence and have his strength to overcome the trials of life.

When a person receives God's new life into their lives it changes them. Jesus taught his followers the Principles of his Kingdom. (Matt.5). These principles are much higher and bigger than rules. They provide the energy for living in the Kingdom and are the evidence of it. They are principles not laws. Laws are rules that come from the principles which formulate them. Principles are like "keys" that govern the laws. If I give you my keys you would then have access to everything that I have. In a similar way Jesus gives the keys of his Kingdom to those who love and obey him. (Matt. 16:19). They are the keys to every treasure and heavenly promise of God. When you receive Jesus as King and let him live in you, you will experience the principles of the Kingdom flowing through your life and changing you.

The Kingdom of God comes into us. It is not by keeping outward regulations but in righteousness, peace and joy in the Holy Spirit as we trust in Jesus. (Rom. 14:17). The Holy Spirit changes us as we take on the nature of Jesus and his "nature" grows in us. There are nine "fruits of the Spirit" that are mentioned in scripture and they change us from the inside out. (Gal.5:22,23). It is not us trying to change, but God changing us from within. God forms a new nature in us. It takes time to grow and we need to feed the new nature that God has given us. We do this by reading and "digesting" the Word of God, by praying, receiving teaching, and in fellowship and communion with fellow believers. This was what the first followers of Jesus did right from the very start. (Acts 2:42).

Those who obey God in this way are blessed by him. He wants us to be delivered from sin, cleansed from addictions and their consequences, and to live as his child. He wants us to have lasting peace and joy as we live in obedience to his Word and Spirit. He wants us to be filled with his Spirit. His Kingdom is a beautiful place in which to live, far more beautiful than anything else on earth, and Jesus is the King of Peace. He offers his Kingdom to us, and those who are determined to have it press into it. (Luke 16:16). It should be sought with determination and commitment. Those who seek it may experience setbacks and even persecution but it is worth it for it is the only life that is worthwhile.

We will have an abundant entrance into the everlasting Kingdom of the Lord Jesus Christ as the virtues of Christ's own divine nature, such as love, joy, peace, longsuffering, kindness, goodness, faithfulness, humility and self-control, grow in us. (2 Pet. 1:11). These are the evidences of God's Kingdom. Many people, young and old, are lonely, empty and discouraged, and desperately seek meaning and fulfillment in their lives. Only Christ gives the "water of eternal life" which fully satisfies our every need. (John 4:13,14).

<u>When the life of Jesus</u> comes into us, we are able to share it with others. He gives us the "keys" of his Kingdom so that we can enjoy it and also make it available to others. He came to open the Kingdom to the lost. The very first thing he said in Mark's Gospel was *"Repent, for the Kingdom of God is at hand"*. (Mark 1:15). He declared the Kingdom to the poor and needy, and healed the sick and broken-hearted, and delivered those bound by Satan. Every time he healed the sick or did a miracle, he reached into the future Kingdom age and released its dynamics into the present age, to bring healing, deliverance and life. He superimposed the future age upon this age. He uses those who believe in him, to do the same. (Matt. 10:5-8). With his authority they can share his Kingdom with those who need help,

bringing hope and life to prisoners lost in sin. (Mark 16:15-18). The Gospel of God's Kingdom has the power to save sinners and change communities and nations. The Gospel is the only hope for a lost world, not philosophies or religions, and we have the responsibility to share it to all who are willing to listen.

GOD'S KINGDOM WILL FILL THE EARTH (Psalm 22:27,28)

Jesus prayed, *"Thy Kingdom come, Thy will be done"* and said we should pray in the same way. He brought the Kingdom and made it available to all who receive it through repentance and faith. He also prayed for it to prevail on earth. Christ made very clear that he would return as King of Kings and one day fully establish his reign on earth. (Matt. 25:31). He foretold that before that happens there will be worldwide proclamation of the Gospel to every nation. (Matt. 24:14). He said *"This Gospel of the Kingdom will be preached for a witness to all nations, and then the end shall come."* God is even now setting up his Kingdom and preparing people to be part of it. Despite the sin and confusion, it is coming closer every day.

Many centuries ago, the prophet Daniel foretold that a time will come when God will take control of all nations. (Daniel 7:22). The kingdoms of the earth will pass away and God's Kingdom will be established forever. (Heb. 12:28). This will happen at Christ's return. That event is drawing near. As a woman gives birth, so the Bible says that God's Kingdom will give birth to an age of peace and righteousness. (Isaiah 66:7-19, 30:4-7, 31:35, Rev. 21:2-22:5).

Through the centuries the Kingdom has grown like an embryo hidden from view, invisible, unnoticed. There have been times of trial and persecution and there have been times of great joy as believers "saw" the age to come and leapt for joy just as a baby does in its mother's womb. (Luke 1:41). However, the time for the visible manifestation of God's Kingdom will surely come. With great expectancy we wait for it, as have many men and women through the ages. It is closer now as we enter into the time of final travail of its birth. Out of the suffering and pain of this present age the birth of the Kingdom of God will come upon earth. The kingdoms of this world will not get improve but will be replaced and make way for the Kingdom of Christ. (Rev.11:15). Jesus will return.

<u>When Jesus</u> lived on earth, Satan tempted him by offering him all the kingdoms of the world which he then controlled, but Jesus refused this counterfeit offer. (Matt.4:8,9). He defeated him at the cross, rose from the dead and will return to reign in righteousness over all kingdoms. His Kingdom is far more majestic than anything on earth. When the Queen of Sheba visited Solomon's glorious kingdom, she said that it was far more splendid than what she had been told. (1 Kings 10:7). This is true of Christ's Kingdom. Our minds cannot fully comprehend the things that God has prepared for those who love him, they are beyond description and more blessed than tongue can tell. (1 Cor.2:9).

Two thousand years ago God offered this Kingdom to all who want to be part of it. The offer is still open to you as long as you are willing to receive Jesus as Lord. He came to give abundant life. (John 10:10). If you are outside of Jesus you are outside everything that God wants for you – it means you are spiritually lost, a beggar, and the devil has deceived you. If you receive Jesus you become an heir to his Kingdom and all his infinite riches. (Acts 26:18, Rom. 8:16,17).

If you have never done so before then respond to God's offer. <u>Repent</u> - in other words, recognize your need of Jesus and <u>confess</u> your sins to him. Open your life to him and ask him to enter your heart as Saviour and King. <u>Trust</u> him to forgive you. By receiving him you will become a child of God and experience spiritual <u>rebirth</u>, you will be born into God's family, and receive eternal life. (John 1:12,13, 3:16,17). You will be fully adopted as <u>God's own child</u>. You will also become a <u>citizen</u> of God's eternal Kingdom. This is not joining a denomination but receiving Jesus as your Lord. It is receiving God's perfect purpose for your existence and his promise of <u>eternal life</u> in a heavenly home that is beyond your ability right now to imagine.

<u>Repentance is not mentioned much in churches today but it is the key to everything God wants you to have</u>: no other key opens his Kingdom.

CHAPTER 2 – TWO KINGDOMS - one of Light and one of Darkness

There are two invisible kingdoms working in the world. One is the Kingdom of God and the other is the kingdom of Satan. God is Light, Satan is darkness. The Bible reveals God as pure, loving, kind, and merciful, and Satan as evil, hateful, merciless and cruel. God loves you, the devil hates you.

Many people deny the existence of a devil but serve him nevertheless, some knowingly, some unawares, and millions are enslaved by him. There is plenty of evidence for him all around us. You may not know it but you are in a war with him and he is your archenemy and will do everything possible to destroy you. God is your Creator and has done everything to save you. Satan is against you God is for you. The Bible says there is one God – the Almighty, self-sufficient, all wise, omnipotent, omniscient, omnipresent, eternal, infinite, loving God. He existed before the world was made and is the Creator who made all things. (Genesis 1:1, John 1:1-18). The devil is a counterfeit and is called the "god of this age" and throughout history has deceived mankind. (2 Cor. 4:4). Jesus taught that there are two kingdoms: one is the Kingdom of God and his angels; the other is the kingdom of Satan and his demons. These two kingdoms are at war and influence this world and everyone in it.

The Bible tells us that Satan has deceived both men and angels. He is a malevolent being who, disguised in the form of a serpent, misled people to disobey the Lord. He destroyed the harmony in the Garden of Eden and by sin and death robbed us of life. (Genesis 3:1-8). *spirit of* *The Serpent*

The origins of Satan are shrouded in mystery. Long ago Satan rebelled against God and was subsequently cast out of heaven. There are ancient texts that tell of a rebellion among heavenly beings and in the Old Testament there are two references to it. The first is given by the Biblical prophet Isaiah. (Isaiah 14:12-15). He linked it with the ancient king of Babylon who was filled with pride. Evidently this man was only a pawn in the power of Satan who sought to overthrow God and said he would dethrone God and exalt himself above him and take his place. Note that Satan said in his heart that he would ascend above the heights of the clouds, the cloud of God's glory, exalt his throne above the stars of God, and sit where God sits on the mount of congregation on the farthest sides of the north (this is figurative of where God dwelt in his temple). Satan wanted to be like the "Most High" and attempted to overthrow and replace the Almighty God of heaven. This attempted coup-d'etat failed for God cast him out of heaven.

The second reference is given by the Biblical prophet Ezekiel who described an imposing being known as a "cherub" who empowered the proud Phoenician king of Tyre. (Ezk. 28:12-17). This king was an earthly man but the narrative describes a spiritual power behind his throne, the "anointed overshadowing Cherub", a unique and beautiful being who was the "sum of perfection, wisdom and beauty", one of the most powerful beings that has ever existed. He was originally very close to God with the responsibility of ministering personally to him. Both Isaiah and Ezekiel described the same being. His great wealth and power filled him with ambition and pride and he rebelled against God. He was originally blameless and perfect in all his ways *until sin was found in him*. God never made anything imperfect or sinful. Nevertheless, every living being has a free will and this Cherub sinned. Satan is the originator and source of all sin. Sin cannot remain in the presence of a Holy God and this cherub was cast out of heaven. Although God did not immediately destroy him, sin is self-destructive and is like a "fire" from within that eventually destroys all who sin (Ezk.28:18,19). God in his foreknowledge knew this and foreordained, from the foundation of the world, that his own Son, Jesus Christ, would overthrow Satan and destroy his work. (John 16:11, 1 Pet. 1:20, Acts 2:23).

God did not make press-button robots when he made humans. God is a God of love and he made beings who like him were capable of loving. He made them in his own image and capable of choosing. This required they have free will for without it one cannot love; only beings with freedom to choose can love. When God gave the power of choice to his creation, to great and powerful beings as well as man, it allowed the possibility of rebellion and for sin to enter.

Satan is called the "god of this age" and he will be judged, bound and destroyed, never again to exist in the eternal realms of God. That was why Jesus came: to destroy the power of Satan. (1 John 3:8). Sin, death, rebellion, pain, fear and every other evil thing will never enter the Kingdom of God. Those who live in Heaven will never again experience any of these things because sin and Satan will be destroyed forever. "There will be no more death or tears…for the former things have passed away". (Rev. 21:4).

Jesus called Satan the "prince of this world" and in the New Testament he is called "the adversary". (John 12:31, 14:30, 1 Tim. 5:14, 1 Pet. 5:8). When Jesus hung on the cross Satan attacked him with every possible onslaught. Alone and without using his divine powers Christ withstood all the evil that Satan threw at him. The Lord, as a man, was beaten beyond recognition and mentally tormented beyond all others but he withstood the full force of evil and defeated it. At the cross Satan was defeated and is now doomed for utter destruction. Jesus destroyed him by shedding his own blood and laying down his own life. (Heb.2:14,15, 9:11-14, 13:12, 20, Acts 20:28).

SEVEN JUDGMENTS ON SATAN

There are seven progressive judgments on Satan: some have already happened and some are still to come.

1/ Ezekiel 28:16 – He was cast out from God's Presence.
2/ Genesis 3:14 – God pronounced judgment on him in Eden.
3/ Luke 10:17-19. Jesus defeated Satan's demons and Satan fell from his position in the heavenly realms.
4/ Col. 2:14,15. Jesus defeated and disarmed him at the cross.
5/ Eph. 2:2,6, 6:12, Rev. 12:7. There is a war now in the "heavenly places" which will end with him being cast down to earth.
6/ Rev. 20:1-3. At the return of Jesus, he will be bound for a thousand years.
7/ Rev. 20:10. His final judgment and total destruction are foretold.

CHAPTER 3 – GOD'S KINGDOM THROUGH THE AGES

The Bible does not tell us when the beginning was but says that God was there in the beginning. (John 1:1-3). God's plan unfolded in a progressive way and will end in a great finale. The number seven is a significant number, for God instituted the first week in the creation account. (Gen. 1). Biblical history, from the beginning of God's dealing with mankind to the end, is laid out over a millennia week in which the Bible message is explained. God controls time and extends or shortens it. *"With the Lord one day is as a thousand years, and a thousand years as one day".* (2 Peter 3:8).

The modern theory of evolution cannot be proven and is used to try and discount a Creator. Time is controlled by God and varies throughout the universe. This is why scientists consider it to be relative and subject to change. God, however, is timeless and dwells in eternity and foreordained all the ages of mankind. In the" beginning" God made time, but God is not bound by it and inhabits eternity; he transcends time at both beginning and end simultaneously. (Psalm 90:2, Isaiah 57:15, Mic.5:2). History is actually His-Story for he planned the course of history, both the start and finish, which will not last millions of years, and according to the first apostles we are already in the "last days". (Acts 2:17, 2 Tim. 3:1, Heb. 1:2, Js. 5:3, 1 Pet. 1:20, 2 Pet. 3:3,4, 1 Jn. 2:18, Jude 18). (See Creation – Notes page 98)

To correctly understand the Bible message, we must remain within the Biblical time reference. The birth of Jesus was exactly at the right time, in the "fullness of time" (Gal. 4:4). God fully controlled the preceding ages and dealt with mankind step by step, preparing mankind for the coming of Christ at the right moment. Through different stages God revealed a progressive plan, from innocence, to sin consciousness, then to understanding his law, and finally to salvation in Jesus.

Since the birth of Christ, over 2000 years has passed during which the Gospel has been declared throughout the world. Jesus said that after the Gospel had been proclaimed to every nation he will return and the end of this present age will occur. (Matt. 24:14). The apostle John said this would be followed by a thousand years in which all nations will submit to the authority of his Kingdom. (Rev. 20:2-6). This future age is the "Kingdom age" and is a forerunner to the ages still to come in which God's Kingdom will endure and endlessly increase. (Matt. 25:34, Isa. 9:7 CJB).

THE FALL OF ADAM AND WHAT FOLLOWED

In Eden where Adam and Eve lived there was no sin, and they enjoyed the blissful condition of absolute **innocence**. We don't know how long this lasted but they were sinless and lived in communion with God. (Gen. 1). By eating from the "tree of knowledge of good and evil" they sinned and their fellowship with God was disrupted and that beautiful state of security, harmony, peace and joy was broken by fear, toil and death. (Genesis 2 & 3).

When sin entered death followed, and affected every living individual and, with no means of redemption, this first age was destined to end in judgment and failure. (Gen.3:14-19). God, however, promised a future Saviour from the "seed" of a woman, in other words, one day another Adam would be born who would overcome death and the curse of sin and, through the resurrection, open a new age of deliverance from death. In the meanwhile, God himself covered man's sin with the skin of an animal slain on their behalf. (Genesis 3:21). This depicted the promise of future deliverance through the "Lamb of God", the Lord Jesus, who would be an atoning sacrifice on our behalf.

THE TIME OF CONSCIENCE

After the fall of mankind another stage developed, the *age* of **conscience**. Because Adam and Eve ate the fruit of the tree of the Knowledge of Good and Evil, sin became universal and death followed. Ever since, every person has the awareness of a God-given conscience, an inborn knowledge of right and wrong, of good and evil no matter how elementary, which makes us morally responsible for all we do to the higher authority of God. All mankind lives by the restraints of this inner conscience as it directs right from wrong. It is our inner compass which convicts us when we commit a wrong deed.

However, instead of listening to this God-given conscience and the conviction that it brought, mankind discarded the conviction of truth it brings and, instead of their conscience directing their thoughts and actions, it malfunctioned and mankind sank into immorality and depravity. In the years that followed humanity was so inclined towards sin that their thoughts became continually evil and violence filled the entire world. (Gen. 6:5-8).

The same pattern of progress is at work today. Children are born and grow up and need to be taught right from wrong. (Gen.18:19, Deut.4:9, 10, 6:6,7). If this is done correctly then their conscience develops into a guiding force, a compass within them to direct their lives. If people refuse to listen to their conscience, they lose all restraint, and all manner of evil has free course with people doing terrible things without having any conviction about them. When a whole society turns away from godly morals then anarchy prevails.

During this first age of mankind there was a division between those who lived uprightly and those who lived wickedly. Those who obeyed God were wonderfully blessed, even living to a very advanced age (Gen. 5:3-32). Eventually, however, mankind became wicked, and only one man, Noah, was found blameless. God decided there was only one solution, the destruction of the wicked. When people deny their Creator and reject their moral compass they sink to the lowest of deeds. That whole age ended in world judgment with the flood sweeping the ungodly away, but God chose Noah, and his family, to safeguard the continuity of humanity. (Gen. 6: 5-13).

ABRAHAM AND GOD'S PROMISE

The Biblical account progressed to the next stage of God's plan. It was to be one of **promise**.

After the flood survivors multiplied very quickly and cities were built and a new world order established. It wasn't too long before people again went astray and started to build a huge tower which they believed would empower them to access the realms of heaven. It was called the Tower of Babel. The builders wanted to exalt themselves and establish world control without accountability to God. (Gen. 11:39). It was the start of self-grandeur and false worship and laid the foundations for humanistic religion and values that are still entrenched in much of today's philosophy and thinking. In order to stop this God disrupted the building and scattered the people who then formed nations, from which all the nations of today have grown. (Gen. 10).

God then proceeded with the next step of his foreordained plan, and that was to call a man who lived in the city of Ur of the Chaldeans. He was Abraham, the "Father of all who have faith". (Gen.12:1-3).

Once again God chose a man and a family and gave a promise to bless and protect him and, through his "seed", bring redemption to all nations of the world. God made an everlasting covenant with Abraham in which his "seed" would bless all the families of the world. (Gen. 17:1-8, 21, Gal. 3:16,17, Heb. 2:16-18). This promise came through Isaac, who represented Jesus: the "seed" God promised as a sacrifice for sin. God promised a Saviour.

Through an extraordinary event, in which Abraham offered Isaac as a living sacrifice, God enacted the future death and resurrection of Jesus Christ. (Heb. 11:17-19). The covenant that God made with Abraham actually foretold God's promise that he would give his own Son as an atoning sacrifice for the whole world. (Jn. 3:16). Jesus was to bear our judgment of sin. God's promise of grace and forgiveness was revealed in Isaac, who represented Jesus. (Gal. 3:5-18, 4:28).

MOSES AND THE AGE OF LAW

Abraham's descendants eventually went into slavery in Egypt. Moses miraculously led the people out of Egypt and God's plan progressed to the next stage: the covenant of God's **Law** established at Sinai. This welded the people into a nation under God, the nation of Israel, which

Commandment
Conviction
Condemnation

was chosen to be the bearer of the message of God's laws to all nations.

The giving of the Law was God's answer to a broken conscience. It reinforced man's conscience by declaring the Ten Commandments of God written in stone. It plainly declared what was right and what was wrong. The first four commandments are to do with our relationship with God and the last six with our fellow man. It was no longer possible to shrug sin off. In a sense we can say that God gave the written law because mankind refused to listen to and respect the inner law written in their hearts. No man now had an excuse for their sin.

The law was given not to save but to convict. (Rom. 3:19,20). It was like a schoolmaster to bring people to repentance and faith. (Gal.3:24-26, Rom. 7:7-13). No one is able to keep the Law of God and it is written "all have sinned and fall short of the glory of God". (Rom. 3:23). No one can therefore be justified by trying to keep the law for it is impossible to do so; all have broken it no matter how good they may appear to be, and sin ends in death. (Rom. 7:9-13).

The Laws of God brought condemnation not life and that age ended in judgment. This was as far as humanity could go: all men were sinners and the result brought death. Despite the great prophets and "Holy men", no one was able to progress further, for this age like the ones before, ended in death. All mankind was under the shadow of death and its darkness. (Lk. 1:79, Rom.5:14). It required a spotless and perfect man to fulfill the Law of God and establish a new covenant, thereby breaking the hold sin had over the whole human race. The law was necessary in order to show us the standards God requires and to lead us into a place in which we can receive the gift of his grace. The Law was necessary to open the next stage of God's plan.

SALVATION THROUGH JESUS CHRIST

When God gave the Law, he gave something else with it. There were two revelations: one was the Law which led to condemnation and the other was the Tabernacle, called the "Tent of Meeting", which showed the way to salvation. God instituted a system of sacrifices as a visual depiction of what was needed to deliver people from sin. It illustrated the plan of salvation through which people were able to acknowledge their sin and have their conscience temporally appeased and their guilt cleansed by sacrificial substitution. (Heb.9:9, 11-14). Thereby it endorsed the promise of **faith** in a future atonement. I believe if people had understood it correctly, they could have lived a life of faith in God. Instead it became a ritual and they ended up making many sacrifices without a changed heart, so God eventually said it had become unacceptable to him. (Hos. 5:6, 6:6, Ps. 40:6, 51:16, Prov. 15:8, Jer. 6:19,20). The people had chosen ritual instead of faith.

Old Testament prophets, however, declared the coming of a Messiah and began to point towards a future "divine servant" who would do the will of God, bear the sins of the world, pay the supreme sacrifice, and bring in the Kingdom of God. (Isaiah 53). Jesus fulfilled these precise predictions and through his sacrifice we are cleansed of sin, and through his resurrection receive eternal life. (Heb. 10:1-14). When Jesus died the veil in the Temple was rent in two indicating the way to God was open and the sacrificial system had ended. (Matt. 27:51). Through his one sacrifice he opened the way into God's **grace**.

As it is written "the law was given through Moses but grace and truth came through Jesus Christ". (John 1:17).

GOD'S PROMISE THROUGH JESUS

Jesus Christ was the only person able to keep and fulfill the Law of God. (1 Cor. 15:45, Gal. 4:4,5). He was born under the Law and as a human being lived, a perfect life; he kept the law and by doing so was able to break through the great barrier it represented. He became the perfect, spotless sacrifice on our behalf. (1 Tim. 2:5, Acts 4:12). Scripture calls him the *last* Adam. (1 Cor. 15:45). The *first* Adam brought death, the *last* Adam brought life. By laying down his perfect life he is able to offer eternal life to all who trust in him. He is the only one who can do this – there will be no more Adams: we either die with the *first* Adam or live with the *last* Adam. He is the "way, the truth and the life". (John 14:6). He opened the new age of the "Covenant of

Grace". Mankind has two representatives, the first Adam and the last Adam, and they represent two alternatives, sin and death or pardon and eternal life to which there are two responses, doubt or faith. The choice is ours which to follow, either to believe God's Word or to doubt it.

Christ offers the only alternative to the death which sin produces and the Law endorses. God offers mercy to all who have faith in Christ. The choice is to either trust in ourselves and our own inadequate efforts which are dismally hopeless, or trust in God's perfect substitute, who took our judgment for us, died for us, came alive for us, and ascended to heaven for us. (Isa. 64:6, Gal. 2:16).

All the previous ages ended in judgment but Jesus took all the judgment on himself. (Isa. 53:4,5). I believe that if he had not died on the cross at that time in history judgment would have fallen upon the world. The history of mankind is one long sordid story of violence, murder, corruption, greed, immorality and all the other broken laws of God, and judgment was inevitable, but Jesus flung himself into the gap and the world was spared at that time. The Black Cloud Is Lifted

It is at the cross that good and evil was judged. It is at the cross where judgment fell. The tree that brought death became the tree of life. It was on the cross that Jesus bridged the immeasurable gap between heaven and earth, satisfied the Law of God, and opened the door of grace. At the cross there is pardon and life instead of death.

GOD'S PLAN FOR THE WORLD AND FOR INDIVIDUALS

All the previous dealings of God with mankind through the ages were in accordance with his foreordained plan to bring salvation.

His Law worked through our conscience and was intended to bring people to repentance and faith in Christ and to make people realize their complete inability and total inadequacy to keep either God's standards of righteousness or their own inner convictions. God's plan for mankind and for every individual is to bring us to a place of faith in him and not ourselves.

Infants born into this world enjoy a time of innocence and are not accountable for past sins. Having been born into Adam's race they have, however, inherited a fallen nature even though they have no personal sin. As they grow, they will normally mature into understanding sin. (Rom. 7:9). The individual's conscience, that instinctive intuitive inner knowledge of good and evil, begins to develop. This is influenced by culture and upbringing and can malfunction but will inevitably shape our values and boundaries. God uses our conscience to convict us of sin (John 8:9) and if we reject that conviction, we will suffer severe consequences, for our sin violates God's Law written not only on stone but in the hearts of all men and women. (Rom. 2:14-16). If people disregard their conscience, they eventually lose all restraint and become "confirmed sinners" and their conscience malfunctions and is seared. (1Tim. 4:2, Titus 1:15).

Our inner conscience is our silent witness to God's laws. When it functions correctly it establishes moral guidelines and brings correction, if individuals listen to it. When a person hears the Gospel and comes to a proper realization of sin it leads them into repentance. True repentance is not a once-off thing but a state of mind that, instead of making excuse or covering up for wrongdoing, leads us into an honest appraisal of our depravity. When a person is convicted of their total inability to change or save themselves, then the Spirit of God can lead them to God's substitute and our mediator, Jesus Christ. This may happen through someone's personal witness, or from a sermon, or by reading the Bible, or in other ways that the Holy Spirit may use. The reaction of a sincere person is then by faith to make a decision and receive Christ as Saviour. (Rom.10:8-17).

When someone believes in Jesus and receives him as their Saviour they experience rebirth by his life-giving Spirit. They pass from death to life. They pass out of guilt and condemnation into the place of God's grace and salvation. Pardon is extended to them through the death, burial, and resurrection of Christ. By receiving him as Lord a transaction takes place. They give up their old life and receive his new eternal life. By identifying with Christ, they are made one with his death and burial and also his resurrection. (Rom. 6:1, Gal. 2:20). This is portrayed in **water baptism**. Through repentance the person dies to sin and self, and their old nature is symbolically buried and they rise in new life. Water baptism is an outward figure and does not save anyone. Nevertheless, it portrays a spiritual reality of what happens when we turn away from ourselves and trust in the Lord Jesus Christ. It is a command and should be obeyed and carries an enormous significance and spiritual impact for the believer.

The new believer is no longer under the age of law but now under grace and is a citizen of the Kingdom of God. This is why Jesus told Nicodemus that no one could enter the Kingdom of God unless they are born of the Spirit. There is no other way but to be born into it. The previous ages all ended in death. That is why we have to be born again as a new creation. (2 Cor.5:17). We must be born into the age of resurrection that gives life and leads to heaven. All those who have progressed along this spiritual journey from conviction, to repentance, to faith in Christ are forgiven and destined for resurrection. (Phil.3:11). All those stuck at another stage have not yet entered eternal life.

Some people in past ages experienced God's grace and mercy by personally trusting in Christ before he actually had come. Abraham the "Father of Faith" had the Gospel preached to him long before Jesus came. He believed and received it by faith. (Gal. 3:6-14, 18 Heb.4:2). Others did too. Moses lived under law but was undoubtedly a man who trusted in grace. David certainly was not saved by keeping the law for he failed terribly. He looked forward to the *future* Messiah and through conviction and repentance put his faith in him. He thereby personally received grace before it was historically fulfilled. Others had the same faith but never saw its full reality and had to wait for it to be fulfilled by Christ. (Heb.11:13, 39,40).

Today we are actually living in the "age of grace" and people have the opportunity to receive God's grace. However, many people have not yet received it because they have not put their faith in Christ. They are currently living in the age of grace but spiritually are back in one of the previous ages and have not entered into grace. When a person denies that they have sinned they are manifesting a complete ignorance of God's law and righteousness – they have not got past the first basic truths. When a person says, "I am good enough", they are fooling themselves and not allowing their God-given conscience to function and discern good and evil. When a person says, "I am able to keep all God's commandments" they are dishonest with themselves and have not yet come to truth and repentance. They are dead in their trespasses and sins. (Eph.2:1)

Only when we are honest about ourselves and face up to our need of salvation can we be delivered from spiritual death and enter the abundant life of God. (John 10:10). Christ came to save the lost, but people need to realize that they are lost. (Luke 19:10).

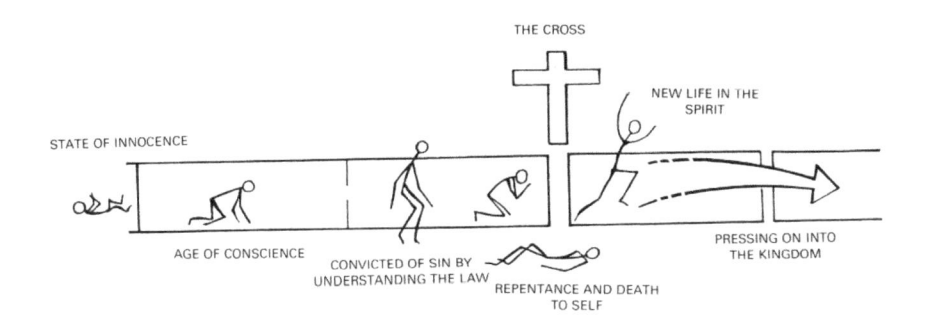

Those who respond to Christ receive his promise of abundant life and pass from the bondage of the old age to the liberty of the new age. They pass from condemnation to forgiveness. They pass from defeat to victory. The sad thing is that some of God's children still live defeated lives, they are saved but not victorious. The Bible has much to say about Christians growing in grace and living in the Spirit. This present age is not yet the "Kingdom Age" but an age of conflict, confusion, persecution, tribulation and trial. We are not yet reigning with Christ for that is a future promise. (2 Tim.2:12, Rev. 5:10 we *shall* reign, future tense; Rev.20:6, 22:5). It is "through much tribulation that we enter the Kingdom of God". (Acts 14:22). It is those who lay down their lives who will reign. (Rev. 12:11). The glory of the Kingdom is still future but believers can see it now just as they did in the days of

Christ. When he came as King, he brought it near. (Mark 1:15 NIV). It is coming closer every day, every moment. This is the real new age under God, not the new age taught from some pulpits.

God's Kingdom, as opposed to mans', will be one of glory, perfection, peace, joy and abundant life. It is possible to "see" it now. When someone in this present age is reborn, filled with the Spirit and delivered from sin, they experience the reality of a future age – the Kingdom Age. Those who deliberately and knowingly reject God's way will not enter and experience God's Kingdom. (Heb.6:4-6).

THE COMING KINGDOM OF GOD

Those who are delivered from sin have been transferred into the Kingdom of God's Son. (Col.1:13). In a spiritual sense they are already in the future Kingdom and are no longer citizens of this age but pilgrims passing through looking for a city with eternal foundations. (Heb. 11:16, 12:22,23). Jude 14

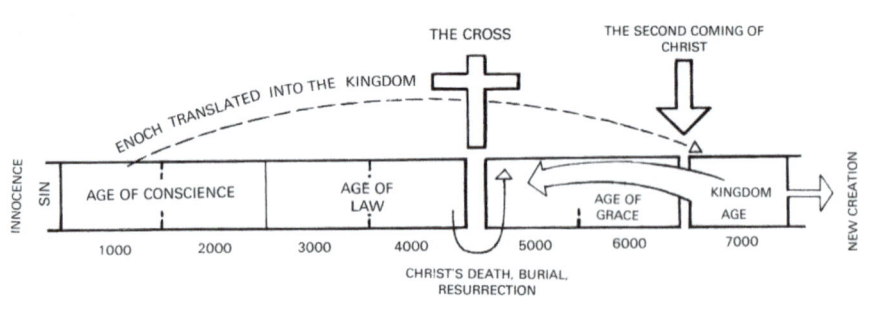

Jesus prayed, "Thy Kingdom come, thy will be done, on earth as it is in heaven". The actual "Kingdom Age" is future but we can press into it, take hold of it and live in it by faith. (Matt. 11:12, Phil. 3:14). We are urged by the Lord to "seek first the Kingdom of God" and all other things will fall into place. (Matt. 6:33). The believer must, therefore, be determined to set their heart on things above and to press against all obstacles towards the coming Kingdom. It is possible even in this age of darkness to live in the age to come. Enoch lived before the flood but saw the Lord coming with ten thousand angels. (Heb. 11:5, Jude 14,15). Jesus said that some of the disciples would not die until they saw the Kingdom of God. (Luke 9:27).

There is a spiritual progression through the ages of mankind. It started with innocence, then conscience was awakened within individuals and society, this developed into understanding right and wrong and God's Law which brought condemnation and death, but it was given to lead into repentance and truth, and open the way for grace to reign in righteousness.

This is what Jesus offered when he said "*Repent for the Kingdom of God is at hand*". Through his death he opened the way of forgiveness to all who choose to live in God's Kingdom and, although the fullness of the Kingdom is still future, we can see and enter it now through faith in Jesus the King. That does not mean we suddenly become wealthy and prosperous in this world's riches, quite the opposite, it may mean we have to take up the cross and be persecuted, tested and even suffer but we will have the assurance of God's love and eternal life. (Matt.10:16-39, 16:24-28).

THE CROSS OPENS THE WAY INTO THE KINGDOM

When it came time for Jesus to go to the cross he said, "Now is the world judged". The entire world and everyone in it will be judged at and by the cross. In other words, everyone will be accepted or rejected by their response to the cross. The true gospel is about the cross which stands at the focal point of history. Sooner or later everyone will be confronted with it. Everyone's journey leads eventually, in one way or another, to the cross. The everlasting Gospel is the Gospel of the cross which will be preached to all mankind. (Rev.14:6). What people do with it will determine their eternal destiny.

This was dramatically portrayed when Jesus died on the cross. On each side of him was a condemned sinner. They saw him die and both mocked him. However, one repented and called out to Jesus, "Lord remember me when you come into your Kingdom". Jesus immediately assured him of eternal life. (Luke 23:43). Even this hardened thief found forgiveness. Sooner or later each person will be confronted by the cross. The **cross** stands in the "eternal now". Jesus said that if he "is lifted up" he will draw all men to himself. (John 3:14-18, 12:32). Just as the serpent was lifted up in the wilderness depicting the horror of sin, and all who looked upon it in faith were healed, so too all those who look with faith to Jesus on the cross will be saved. (Num.21:9). If, however, having understood God's offer of clemency an individual turns away from it, they will be lost. (Heb.10:29). By rejecting the sacrifice Jesus made there is no salvation. There is no forgiveness, no redemption, no justification, no sanctification, no peace with God and no eternal life without the **blood**. (Eph.1:7, Col.1:14, 20, Rom.5:9, Heb.10:10, Rev.1:5, 5:9). Yet so many churches today never mention the cross or the blood in their sermons. Christ died for you because he loves you. Search the pages of history and you will not find anyone else who loves you like he loves you. With wide open arms he calls you to come. If you come to him you will be fully forgiven.

No wonder Pontius Pilate pointed to Jesus and said "Behold your King". He was covered with blood after having been scourged. Christ's earthly throne was a cross and his crown a crown of thorns. He was crowned the King of Love. He is incomparable – there is none other as pure and loving as him. He was without sin and never became sin but took the curse of sin and its punishment upon himself. He did an exchange by taking our sins in order to give us his righteousness. (Gal.3:13, 2 Cor.5:21). God was in Christ reconciling the world to himself. (2 Cor.5:18,19). Christ took the consequences of sin and experienced every pain, suffering, sadness and sorrow that the whole of mankind has ever experienced. He took your place so that you may be forgiven, reborn, and receive life.

If, by looking at and considering the suffering that Christ endured on the cross, you glimpse just a fraction of God's great love for you, then it will touch your heart where nothing else does. It will compel you to bow at the feet of Christ, give him your heart, crown him as your king, and motivate you to follow him.

CHAPTER 4 - THE LAWS OF GOD'S KINGDOM

In the Old Testament the citizens of Israel were in a covenant with God through the laws of Moses. In the New Testament the citizens of Heaven are in a covenant with God through the <u>Royal Law</u> of King Jesus. Although many people believed and received Jesus when he came, many clung to their religious rituals and rejected him. (Zech. 9:9, Matt. 21:4-9, Jn. 19:14-22). Religion, with all its traditions and rituals, cannot give life. No religion can do that; only Jesus, who came not to start a religion but to give life. (John 10:10, 14:6, 1 Jn. 5:12). The difference between religion and devotion is that one is lifeless and the other life-giving. Religion crucified Jesus, Jesus gives life.

TWO COVENANTS – COVENANT OF <u>LAW</u> AND COVENANT OF <u>GRACE</u>

There is a law of sin and death, and a law of forgiveness and life: one is the law of rejection and doubt the other the law of belief and faith.

All the cultures of the world are linked to religious philosophy of some kind. This is because all people have some kind of rudimentary knowledge of God. Within mankind is an inborn instinct that witnesses to God and there are numerous religions which express mankind's search for meaning. However, religions do not necessarily present truth about God but distortions and deceptions. Atheists totally discount God's existence, often because of the uncomfortable conviction it brings them or because of the terrible excesses and error they see in religion. The denial of God, however, is a rejection of him for overwhelming evidence confirms his existence. (Rom. 1:19-32). Agnostics on the other hand, are people who "doubt" the existence of God but can give no convincing reason why. The indifference of agnosticism and rejection of atheism both require no faith, just doubt, and illustrate two fundamental laws: the law of doubt and the law of faith. Jesus said to the people of his day, *"you believe in God, believe also in me".* (Jn. 14:1). The way of doubt ends in death. The opposite of doubt is faith and we are exhorted to believe and have faith. *"The fool has said there is no God, but the fear of the Lord is the beginning of wisdom".* (Ps. 53:1-3, 10:4). To reject the Lord who loves us with divine love is a choice. However, to be totally indifferent as to whether he exists or not is possibly the greatest insult we could afford him. The greatest honour we can give anyone is to say, "I believe in you and I trust you with my life". When we say this of God, we are expressing the highest praise, acclamation and respect for him that we can give. When we say it of Jesus, we are opening the door to the greatest power available on earth and the highest authority in heaven. When facing great difficulty, or are in the middle of a storm or terrible trial, and we say we believe in Jesus, we are giving him the greatest compliment possible. The greatest thing anyone can ever do is to believe in Jesus Christ. (Jn. 6:29).

He said, *"The time is fulfilled, and the Kingdom of God is at hand. Repent and believe the Gospel".* (Mark 1:15). It is by believing that we enter the Kingdom. If we doubt, we will never enter or receive anything. Doubt is a block to all that God has promised. It denies his existence, mistrusts his character, and discounts his promises. Doubt is the greatest sin for it prevents us from entering God's Kingdom. (Rev. 21:8). Because of unbelief we are unable to receive God's love and his precious promises. Jesus instructed us to believe in God. (Jn.14:1). Those who believe are saved. (Jn. 1:12). If we believe in God there are no limitations because God has no limitations; nothing is impossible. (Matt. 17:20, 19:26, Luke 1:37, Mark 9:23,24, 11:23,24, John 20:30,31, Heb. 11:6).

God made man in his own image but ever since the fall of Adam man has been trying to make God in his own image and become like him. (Acts 17:29). Mans' ideas about God fall far short of God's perfection. This is why we need a revelation of God and this is found in Jesus who is the "express image" of God. (Heb. 1:1-4).

The Bible is very clear about the deity of Christ. (Col. 1:15-19, 2 Cor. 4:4, John 1:14-18, 1 Tim. 3:16, 6:14-16, Titus 2:13, 3:4, 1 John 5:20, Jude 24,25). All the fullness of the Godhead dwells bodily in him. (Col. 2:9). There are many scriptures that tell of Father, Son and Holy Spirit as the Almighty Godhead. (1 Jn. 5:7,8, Rom. 1:20).

THE GARDEN OF EDEN

Genesis records the original conditions of Eden in the beginning as:

1. The principle of life in fellowship with God.
2. The principle of the existence of good and evil.
3. The principle of temptation and death.
4. The principle of judgment.

Adam had two sons, Cain and Abel. They both brought offerings to God: Abel brought a lamb and Cain brought fruit from the ground. Cain had worked hard to grow the fruit because the ground had been cursed but Abel just brought a kid. The one offering represented Cain's self-effort, the other God's provision. Abel represented the principle of trusting God, and Cain of rebellion against God for he knew the ground was cursed. (Gen. 3:17). The lamb was perfect, the fruit was not. Cain offered self-effort, which represents the way of fallen man and self-grandeur. It is the way of humanity.

This is the way of religion which teach us that by trying our best in our we can improve ourselves and attain the standard we think God wants. It is man trying to reach God, trying to prise open the door and prove our own ability. The Bible teaches the opposite and declares that all men have fallen short of God's standards and are hopelessly lost, unable to attain them. It teaches that we are unable to save ourselves: God needs to rescue us. This teaching is different from all religions. It differs because of the direction. "New Age" teaching is the exaltation of man, Christ's is the exaltation of God.

GOD IS HOLY – MAN IS SINFUL

God is absolutely holy and morally upright, free from sin, and blameless in all he does. He sets the standards and laws for the whole of the universe. These laws don't just govern the physical laws of creation but also the moral laws of mankind. The universe is a "moral universe" because its creator and maintainer is a moral being, and fallen mankind is unable to attain the kind of righteousness that is required to have fellowship with him. Some people may live better lives than others but, in some way, all break his law. (James 2:10,11). If the pass mark for an examination is 50% and one candidate achieves 1% and another 49%, they have both failed. God's pass mark cannot be lowered: it is 100%. All of us fall short of it.

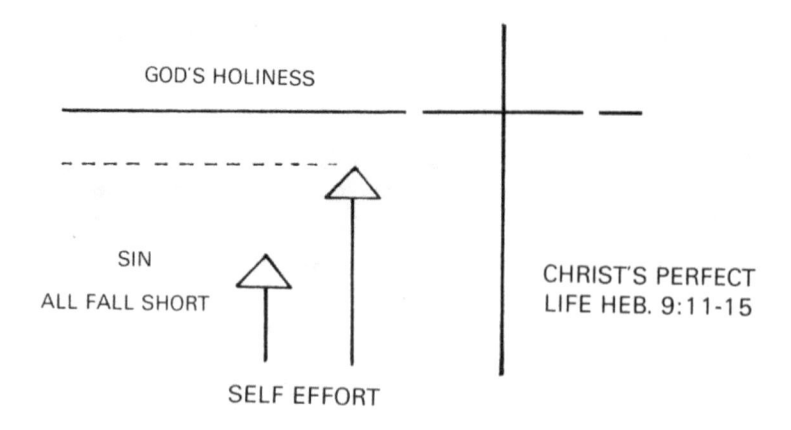

```
                GOD'S HOLINESS                    |
      _____           ____  _ _|_ _ _
                                                  |
      - - - - - - - - - △                         |
                                                  |
           SIN         △                  CHRIST'S PERFECT
       ALL FALL SHORT  ↑                  LIFE HEB. 9:11-15
                       |                          |
                       |                          |
                    SELF EFFORT
```

Because of the sin factor no one can attain God's standard despite their best efforts, intelligence, or skill. The gulf is too wide for fallen man to span. All fail. Christ, however, came from heaven and was perfectly one with the Father and perfect in all his life. (Heb.9:11-15).

CHRIST IS MEDIATOR

Because of God's loving kindness and tender mercies God himself spanned the gulf by sending his Son from heaven. Jesus came from God as "Son of God" and "Son of Man", God in union with man, "Immanuel", God with us. All God's attributes are found in Christ, yet he was truly human. He is God and man, in one person. In the New Testament he is called the Son of God over 44 times and the Son of Man over 59 times. The fullness of God was *in* Christ reconciling the world to himself. (Col. 2:9, 2 Cor. 5:19).

Christ did what no other man could do: he never sinned. By not doing so he lifts all who forsake their own effort and put their trust in him, above the impossible barrier and into union with God. He became the immaculate mediator between God and us. (1 Tim. 2:1-6). Because he is both God and man, he is the divine bridge.

It is only through Christ that we are acceptable to God. There is no "religion" that offers such a personal substitute. Christianity is totally unique in this respect, which sets it apart from all others and provides the only possible way to God. Christ alone is the way to heaven: he is the ladder which spans the gulf between a Holy God and lost mankind. (John 1:51, Genesis 28:12). Jesus said "No man cometh unto the Father except by me". (John 14:6).

THE ROYAL LAW – Matthew 22:36-40, 1 John3:23

The Old Testament is full of rules and commandments. The people were under the law and without further revelation were in bondage to it. It was not possible for them to keep it or fulfill the requirements of the law because they were unable to tackle them from the right direction. They had to be lifted "above the law" in order to keep it. They had to be changed from slaves to children.

The laws of Moses were actually derived from higher principles that affirm and govern them. For example, the law forbade the killing of anyone. The outworking of the real issue is to love our fellow man. If one truly loves others then one will do them no harm. This is the principle upon which the statement is based. This is why Jesus always taught the principle and took it to extreme when he said one should love one's enemies even to laying down one's life for them. When Jesus was asked which was the greatest commandment, he did not quote from the ten commandments but from two lesser-known verses which emphasize the importance of love for both God and man. (Matt. 22:37-40, Mark 12:28-31, Deut. 6:5 and Lev. 19:18). They show that if one does not have a proper relationship with God it is impossible to relate properly to others because both are linked.

Jesus gave the two greatest commands, which are actually spiritual principles. Rules are derived from principles and Jesus always taught the principles. The principle from which a rule or law arises is far more important than the law. If we live in the principles the rules will follow automatically.

Through rebirth Jesus changes the status of believers from slaves to children and elevates us into the realm of principles instead of law. He thereby lifts us out of the bondage of law into the freedom to cherish and enjoy the principles. Slaves are compelled to obey the laws of their master, whereas children choose out of love to keep the commands of their father. As children of God we are delivered from bondage into liberty. (Gal. 3:21-29). Christ taught two great principles from which all others stem. Jesus said that all that is written in the law and the prophets are summed up by just two commandments. The first is in a vertical plane – love for God. The second is in a horizontal plane – love for fellow humans. They form the principles of Christ's Royal Law of love upon which every action will be weighed. (James 2:12). Both these commandments are impossible to keep under duress, only by a freewill choice on our part.

THE DIRECTION OF THE CROSS

CHRIST, MEDIATOR 1 TIM. 2:15

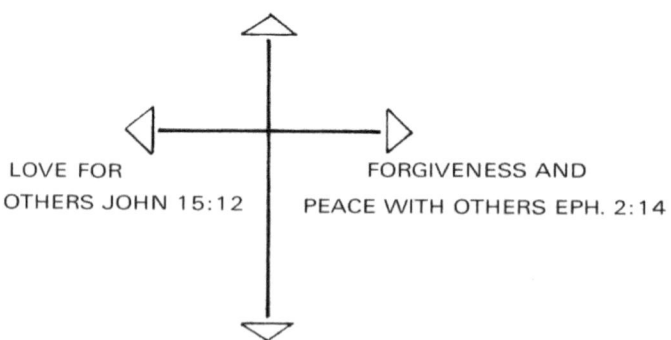

LOVE FOR OTHERS JOHN 15:12

FORGIVENESS AND PEACE WITH OTHERS EPH. 2:14

THE LOVE OF GOD REACHING DOWN TO MAN JOHN 3:16

This is the Royal Law of God's Love.

Instead of giving Ten Commandments Jesus gave two Principles to live by. (John 13:34, 15:9-12):

1/ <u>To Love God</u>. This arises from God's love for us and our response to him. (1 Jn. 4:10-21). God is the originator of love, for he loved us so much that he sent his Son to rescue us. (Rom.5:8). He initiated love to us and we can respond to it. (Jn. 3:16). Because God loved us first, we can love him in return. This is portrayed in the diagram by the vertical line of the cross. It is at the cross that God's love came down from heaven to earth and the way is now open for us to love him back. The cross allows a two-way love.

2/ <u>To Love others</u>. This also arises from God's love and is portrayed by the horizontal line of the cross. Jesus was crucified with his arms wide open to welcome all who come to him. We can only show our love for God in practical terms by loving others: our neighbors and even our enemies. Our love for God reaches out on a horizontal level to those around us. In this way the love of God fulfills the law of God. (Rom. 13:10, Gal. 5:13,14).

Through God's love we are able to keep God's law. The only way is to go via the right route: we first receive God's love and then we are able to let that love overflow to others. This was demonstrated at the cross. Jesus first dealt in a vertical direction by interceding with the Father. He cried "Father forgive them" and thereby raised a ladder to heaven which opened the vertical route. Thereafter he built a bridge on the horizontal level by answering the repentant sinner dying next to him and assuring him, "today you will be with me in paradise".

This forms the cross. Both principles are inter-related. Both depend upon the other. Take one away and there is no cross. The cross forms a ladder to reach God and a bridge to reach our fellow man. Jesus said he was the ladder by which angels would ascend and descend from heaven to earth. (Jn. 1:51, Gen. 28:12).

Christ lifts us above the crossbar into a place where instead of having the oppressive demands of the law bearing down upon us, we can enjoy the freedom of responding in faith to the forgiveness and liberty of God that flows freely from his grace and not his condemnation. (Jn. 8:32-36).

THE BEATITUDES - The Sermon on the Mount.

It is only when Christ is crowned as King within our hearts that we are able to live by the Royal laws of his Kingdom. His Kingdom comes into us and grows in ever increasing ways. Only then do the principles Jesus taught in the Sermon on the Mount become realistic. By revealing the principles of Old Testament laws Christ showed his disciples the futility of trying to keep the laws without a changed heart. He raised God's Laws into the principles from which they originate and made them his commands. (Matt. 5:3-7:29).

When Christ is Lord within a heart there is a changed heart. As the apostle Paul wrote, the Kingdom of God is not necessarily what is done outwardly with an appearance of righteousness, but what is inward. (Rom. 14:17). Outward religion, whether keeping traditions, customs or rules, is only a copy of the self-righteous religion of the Pharisees. Christ delivers us from the trap of self-righteousness into heart-righteousness.

Note how in his sermon Christ contrasted the characteristics of his Kingdom with those of the world. They are diametrically opposed. Worldly kingdoms, whether religious or secular, are based on riches and wealth, power and might. In contrast his Kingdom is one of grace, and favour, to the poor in spirit, to those who mourn, to the meek, and those who hunger and thirst after God's righteousness. Unlike the passing show of worldly pride God's Kingdom brings lasting riches of forgiveness, mercy, comfort and care of others, even to the very lowest, poorest and most insignificant.

The values that Jesus taught cannot be attained through natural means but require a different attitude. Blessed are those who are **poor** for theirs is the Kingdom of Heaven. Blessed are those who **mourn** for they shall be comforted. Blessed are the **meek**, for they shall inherit the earth. Blessed are they who **hunger** and thirst for righteousness, for they shall be satisfied. Blessed are the **merciful**, for they shall obtain mercy. Blessed are the **pure** in heart, for they shall see God. Blessed are the **peacemakers**, for they shall be called sons of God.

Blessed are those who are **persecuted**, for theirs is the Kingdom of Heaven. These seven beatitudes are attitudes that produce great blessing and are very different from the values of the world. They are not self-elevating but self-humbling. The principles of God's Kingdom are necessary to live successfully in God's Kingdom. We hear so much today about getting rich and wealthy, popular and successful, and of being happy and fulfilled, but very little about being poor in spirit, meek and humble. Have we got the right Gospel?

So much of present attitudes are built on putting ourselves first and on "our rights" but that was not what Jesus stood for. He said if someone strikes us, we are to turn the other cheek. (Matt. 5:39). If someone wants to take our coat, we should give him our suit as well. (Matt. 5:40). If someone forces us out of our way, then we are to go twice as far with them. (Matt 5:41). One does not hear this sort of teaching in churches, certainly not much in the western world which seems often preoccupied with success, wealth and self fulfilment.

Jesus continued his sermon by expounding the Old Testament Laws. Far from cancelling them he expanded them. The first was on *murder* and he said it came from disrespect and hate. Then he talked about *adultery* and said it came from lust in the heart. Again, he spoke of *false witness* and implied it came out of pride. He spoke of *revenge*, and retaliation, and said one should respond with forgiveness. He taught on prayer and emphasized the necessity for us to forgive. He went on to comment on other issues. He said that a person is known by the fruit they bear. The apostle Paul summed up the fruits of the Holy Spirit. (Gal. 5:22-25). Perhaps one word that best sums them up is **humility.** (1 Pet. 5:5, Matt. 23:12, Js. 4:6,10, Isa. 57:15, Mic. 6:8). Humility is the hallmark of all great men and women.

The teachings of Jesus are different from those of the world and he concluded by saying that in order to live his way we need to build our lives upon the rock that is himself; the immovable, changeless **"Rock of Ages" Jesus Christ**. (Matt. 7:24-27, Jn.13:15, Js.5:10, 1 Pet.2:21,). His life fully expressed his teaching and he is our supreme example.

CHAPTER 5 – PRINCIPLES FOR LIFE IN CHRIST

Christ taught spiritual truths which, when followed, lead to a full life for those who follow him. The principles we have discussed so far are summarized in the epistle to the Hebrews and are presented there as seven principles to guide us in our following of Jesus, both as individuals and also as a corporate body. (Heb.5:9-6:1,2). Practicing these principles will lead us into a full experience of God's purposes in our lives and churches. They are to help us grow into spiritual maturity. Sadly, they are neglected or even eradicated from the Gospel message of today and often even reversed by the popular "new age gospel" now prevalent. They are called the "**first principles of the Word of God**". The writer of Hebrews addressed baby believers who don't grow because of lack of understanding and application of these principles in their lives. These believers need to grow up and graduate from milk to feed upon the deeper truths of God's Word.

1 - REPENTANCE

[BELIEVE]

The first principle of God's Word is repentance, but not just repentance from our sins but repentance from our "dead works".

Repentance means "*a change of mind*" and "dead works" means "*works of self-justification*". So, the first principle of God is for us to have a change of mind about ourselves and our attempts to justify ourselves: all those things that we do to mask the fact that we are sinners or use as excuses for our sin or to conceal our true depravity. They include all our attempts of self-effort to justify ourselves. Few churches teach on repentance and because of this, conversions are not based on sound Biblical principles but are often shallow transitional experiences based on emotional decisions or wrong concepts.

The Bible teaches that men and women are made in the image of God and must take responsibility for their sin. However, most people play down sin and attempt to excuse themselves. This is not helpful when it comes to salvation for our hearts are very deceptive. God will not compromise with sin and has himself provided the only means for us to be delivered from it, the sacrifice of Christ. However, to benefit from this great sacrifice we must come to a place where we recognize, acknowledge, and confess our condition. Once we do so God cancels our sin and totally eliminates it on the basis that Christ paid for them.

The opening words of Jesus were a call to repentance. Very few people would claim they have lived exemplary lives and most admit that they have failed in one way or another. Many recognize this and try to make amends by "turning over a new leaf" and living "good lives". This alone cannot cancel sin. All our efforts to earn approval, to be acceptable to God, are what the Bible calls "dead works" of self-justification. The Bible says that "all our righteousness is as filthy rags" and "all have sinned and fallen short". (Isa. 64:6, Rom. 3:10,23). No matter how we clothe ourselves in respectability we cannot justify ourselves and have no righteousness of our own.

Jesus told a story about a Pharisee (a religious man who trusted in himself) and a tax collector (considered one of the worst sinners). (Luke 18:9-14). It illustrates what God thinks about self-righteousness. Repentance is more than penance – it is a complete change of mind about oneself. To change one's mind about sin is only half repentance. It is a start but incomplete. Jesus meant more than this: we must turn from ourselves and rely wholly on him.

God desires all people to fully repent. (2 Peter 3:9, Rom. 2:4, Acts 17:30). He does not want any to perish and has no pleasure in the destruction of the wicked. (Ezekiel 18:31,32). He so loved the world and everyone in it that he sent Jesus to save the lost. (Rev. 22:17). Jesus did his part; our part is to repent. (Luke 13:3,5). Many people harden their hearts and resist the Holy Spirit. Others consider themselves to be "good enough" and in no need of salvation. (Acts 7:51, Matt. 9:13). Many try to justify themselves by being good.

Hebrews 9:14 declares that the blood of Christ purges our conscience from "dead works". The spotless Son of God shed his blood and made atonement for our sin. His work is complete and we cannot add to it only accept it. (Heb. 1:3, Rom. 5:8-11). So, we must have a change of mind not only about sin but about ourselves. Christ alone justifies us, just as if we had *never* sinned! Salvation is a gift received through faith. Repentance leads to confession, which opens the way for us to receive forgiveness and every other blessing from God. Repentance is not a once-off event but a way of living; we live in repentance and our attitude is one of repentance. Repentance must guide our thoughts and actions *for the rest of our lives*. It is our foundation.

2 – <u>FAITH TOWARDS GOD</u>

<u>The second principle of God's Word is faith</u>. What is faith? Faith is not knowledge *of* God but trust *in* God. I may know how a parachute works and I may even believe it does but I may not be willing to put my trust in it. Faith in God is my personal trust in him. It is not just faith but faith *towards* God. This is not faith in the numerous gods of the religions that people follow but faith towards the one supreme God and Father of Jesus Christ. Genuine faith is to be sure of the things we hope for and to be certain of the things we cannot see, based on God's Word. It is by faith that people gain God's approval. (Heb. 11:1,2).

<u>Jesus said</u>, *"Let not your heart be troubled: believe in God, believe also in me".* (John 14:1). What wonderful words! First, we believe in God and then we put our faith in him. Faith towards God is not faith in religion or church membership. Neither is it trusting ourselves to live a "good life". As we have seen, everything we do to try to justify ourselves is worthless. It is not self-confidence but God-confidence. Faith's foundation is the integrity of God. It is trusting God alone and what he has done through Jesus Christ. Faith is first and foremost *active*. We have all seen a young child jump into the outstretched hands of their father. The child puts faith in the father and jumps. Faith in action is when you jump into the hands of God. Once having jumped the child allows their father to hold them, without kicking or screaming and relaxes and enjoys the security of the father's arms. The child becomes *passive* in trusting. Faith is first *active* and then *passive*. Faith in action is when I believe God and cast myself upon his mercy. Faith in rest, is when I rest in his promises and trust his faithfulness. (Deut. 33:27). This is the "rest of faith", the *passive* side of faith.

Faith in what God is going to do - Heb. O. Test.
Faith in what God has done.   Heb. N. Test

There is a tendency by some to think of faith as a means to receive things from God, but faith is far more than just a method of receiving things or having prayers answered. Faith must go deeper. It is <u>a way of life</u> which pleases God. "<u>The just shall live by faith</u>". (Hab. 2:4, Rom.1:17, Gal. 3:11,12). *"Without faith it is impossible to please Him, for he who comes to God must believe that He is, and that He rewards all who diligently seek Him"*. (Heb. 6:11).

Faith towards God is placing our faith in what he has done through Jesus Christ. (1 Peter 1:21). God revealed himself through his Son, and faith in him enables us to have a meaningful relationship with God. We are able to approach God through him at any time or situation. Faith is the only way we can approach God, for he cannot be understood with our intellect, or be grasped through our knowledge, and he cannot be appeased by our works. It is by faith alone that we come to him, trusting in Jesus his Son who made the way possible for us to believe. (Heb.10:22).

Faith in Christ is the bedrock of all we believe in and hope for. He is the everlasting Rock of ages upon which we stand. He is the "author and finisher of our faith". (Heb. 12:2). Faith in Christ enables us to live a life pleasing to God. (Heb. 10:38, 11:5). The law does not work through faith but produces "<u>works of the flesh</u>". Whatever is not of faith is sin and these works are called "<u>dead works</u>" because they cannot save but produce death. They are "<u>works of the law</u>". (Gal. 2:16, 5:19-21, Eph. 5:3,11, Rom. 9:30-33, Rom. 14:23, Titus 3:5).

True faith, however, produces <u>works of faith</u> which are called "<u>good works</u>". (Js. 2:14-26, 1 Pet.2:12). The true "<u>work of faith</u>" is not work but belief. (Rom. 3:21-27, 4:2,3, 11:6). Jesus said, *"This is the work of God, that you <u>believe</u> in Him whom He sent"*. (John 6:29, 1 John 3:23). Belief in God is our "work of faith". (1 Thes.1:3). Faith is therefore both active and passive. By faith we do certain things: we believe, we act, and we do <u>good works</u>. True faith always motivates us to do "good works": what we do because we believe in God, not to prove ourselves to him. By faith we also *don't* do certain things: we do *not* deliberately sin or trust in ourselves, but trust in God.

A life of faith enables us to live and die in faith. (Heb. 11:5). This is not necessarily as a martyr, for we will all face death one day. I have, however, seen people face death with great faith, without wavering. The greatest culmination to life is to be numbered with the great men and women who by faith have gone before us. (Heb. 11:13). It is our faith that overcomes the world and it is our faith that enables us to both live and die for Christ. (1 John 5:4,5).

<u>Jesus encouraged</u> his disciples to have faith and asked them why they had so little of it. He said to them, *"Have faith in God"*. (Mark 11:22). He himself lived by faith. That is why God the Father could say of him, "This is my beloved Son in whom I am well pleased". Everything that Jesus did was by faith and obedience to the Father. (John 5:19).

The apostle Paul wrote, "it is no longer I who live, but Christ lives in me, and the life which I now live…I live by faith in the Son of God…(Gal.2:20). The CJB says, "The Messiah lives in me, and the life I now live in my body I live by the same trusting faithfulness that the Son of God had". In other words, Christ's life and faith is *in* us.

Faith will *always* be tested, for that is the nature of it. Faith trusts in the midst of trials. The great apostle Peter wrote that we are "kept through faith, which is more precious than gold", and the end of faith is our salvation. (1 Peter 1:5-9).

Some Christians say they trust God but have never really put their faith wholly in him. They are not sure whether they are forgiven, or if they are born again, or even if they are going to heaven. Others are always anxious, doubtful and fearful. Repentance from dead works and faith toward God go together and dynamically change us into men and women of faith. Laying the foundation of repentance is the key.

Here are some scriptures for your personal study.
Repentance and faith – Acts 20:21.
The Breastplate of Faith – 1 Thes.5:8.
The Fight of Faith – 1 Tim.6:12, 2 Tim.4:7.
The Prayer of Faith – James 5:15.

The Word of Faith – Rom. 10:8.
The Walk of Faith – 2 Cor.4:7.
The Rest of Faith – Heb. 4:3.
The Works of Faith – Js. 2:14-26

3 – INSTRUCTION ABOUT BAPTISMS

The third principle of God's Word is Baptisms. Note that this scripture talks of "baptisms": there is more than one baptism.

Ephesians 4:5, however, speaks of <u>one</u> baptism and this is **water baptism** which is a symbolic enactment of a spiritual reality. Although outward it is an important spiritual act of obedience and expresses **seven** different aspects of truth. The Biblical word for baptism means to be submerged or "be put into something so as to be one with it". It also has the meaning of cleansing and sanctification. Water baptism is a far cry from how most churches conduct it today with their historical tradition that reduces baptism to a worthless unbiblical ritual.

Water baptism is done in the name of the Father, Son and Holy Spirit and identifies the new believer with other believers. It is a public proclamation of our faith and obedience in Christ. (Matt. 28:19). To be true to the meaning of the word and the original manner in which it was done by the disciples and the early believers, it should be by full immersion, and is only for those mature enough to have repented and personally placed their faith in Christ. Peter commanded sinners to "<u>repent and be baptized</u>". (Acts 2:37,38, 8:38).

Baptism by immersion is a command of Christ and necessary for all believers. It is an act of obedience and opens the way for several amazing spiritual realities to be fulfilled in us. Jesus himself humbled himself in baptism and is an example of obedience to God's Word instead of traditions of men. When water baptism is obeyed it brings release from spiritual bondage and facilitates rapid spiritual growth.

As already said, baptism means "to be put into something so as to become fully identified and one with it". It is to be joined in oneness, an in-grafting. Christ was himself baptized but his outward act had a different application for him than for believers. The baptism that Jesus experienced with John the Baptist was different in meaning from the baptism that is done by believers. John's baptism was a baptism of repentance from sin. He called people to repent and confess their sins and to symbolically wash in baptism. Sinners flocked to the River Jordan and went into the water spiritually unclean and came out symbolically clean. (John 1:15-34). Jesus, however, was sinless, had no sin and needed no washing or repentance. John knew this and was reluctant to baptize him. Nevertheless, Jesus told John to baptize him because it "fulfilled all righteousness". What did he mean?

When Jesus was baptized, he went into the river clean and came out carrying the sins of the world. He never became sin but became the sin bearer. John immediately declared him to be the "Lamb of God who takes away (bears away) the sins of the world". (John 1:29). What Jesus did spiritually was to pick up the sins that sinners had washed off in the river. Jesus identified with sinners so as to do an *exchange*: his righteousness for our sins. He was baptized for us and became partaker in our cares and sorrows. (1 Peter 2:22-24, 2 Cor. 5:21, Matt. 8:17, Isaiah 53). He was immersed into humanity and made one with us so as to take our sin upon himself and suffer our judgment in our place on the cross as the Lamb of God. He bore the sins of the whole world and took all our judgment so that we could take his righteousness.

When we get baptized it is opposite to what Jesus did; he identified with us and our sins, we identify with him and his righteousness. He was baptized into our condemnation and death; we are baptized into his righteousness and resurrection. We thereby receive a new spirit, the Spirit of Christ. (Rom.8:9-11, Gal.4:6,7). This does not all happen at baptism but at conversion when the spiritual transaction takes place between Christ and the believer and the result is being born again and receiving eternal life. Christ comes in to us by his Spirit and lives in us. Water baptism outwardly expresses this truth and several other Spiritual truths. There are seven spiritual baptisms.

The first is the baptism of repentance. To receive Christ sinners must first repent. This is a spiritual necessity for all who would receive Christ. In the days of John the Baptist this was expressed in baptism but it must first be an inward experience. We all must repent of sin.

The **second baptism** is to be **baptized into death.** We must turn from the "dead works" which are our own self-efforts for salvation, and die to ourselves and be buried with Christ. The sinner personally identifies with the death of Christ. (Rom. 6:3, Gal. 2:20, Col. 2:11-15). We are baptized into death, but not any death, but "death to sin and self". Water baptism depicts this by the believer being symbolically buried in immersion, and then rising in Christ's new life. We die and rise with Christ. (Rom. 6:1-14). Christ cancelled the law written against us and sets us free. Just as a dead person can no longer die or break any laws, so too we are set free from sin and the law being dead to them. We have been delivered from sin and death. We are no longer "under the law of sin and death" or held in its power, and we are now enabled to live life in the Spirit of Jesus Christ. (Rom. 8:1-14).

Water baptism is a declaration of our turning away from a life of sin and self, and trusting *wholly* in what Christ has done. His grace becomes the means to set us free from the old life of sin. We are no longer "under law but under grace". This does not mean, as some may think, that we are free to continue living in a sinful way but, having died to the old life and the person we used to be, we now live a totally new life free from sin, not free in it.

The third baptism is the baptism into **Christ.** As already explained, we become one with him. (1 Cor. 6:17). Christ lives in us and we live in him. (Gal. 2:19,20). The apostle Paul wrote that "for me to live is Christ and to die is gain". (Phil. 1:21). It is Christ *in* you that is the hope of glory. (Col. 1:27). Because he lives in us by his Spirit, we now have the life of Christ in us and the Spirit of Christ resides in us. (Rom. 8:9,10). One of the proofs of rebirth is a change in life-style.

The fourth baptism is into the **Holy Spirit**. When Christ comes in we are reborn and become a new creation. Once he lives in us by his Spirit, he wants us to live in his Spirit. This is the baptism into the third member of the Godhead, the Holy Spirit. It is seen by some as distinct from one's initial rebirth. I have seen new converts immediately filled with the Holy Spirit after being baptized in water, and I have known others who only experienced this baptism many years after their conversion. Much depends on one's understanding but I have noticed that those who are obedient in full water baptism also experience this baptism quicker than others. Baptism into Christ gives us spiritual life, whereas the baptism in the Holy Spirit gives us the ability to serve him. (Matt. 3:11, Acts 1:5, 8:12-17).

The baptism into the third member of the Godhead is possible through the work of Christ. After a person receives Christ the Holy Spirit becomes their comforter and teacher. He directs and molds them, changing them into the image of Christ. The Holy Spirit strengthens and nurtures the new Christ-life. In this way the believer is empowered by the Spirit to serve Christ. There are nine fruits of Christ's Spirit and there are nine gifts of the Holy Spirit. (Gal. 5:22-26, 1 Cor. 12:7-10). The fruits of the Spirit are listed in three groups: love, joy and peace are to enjoy; patience, kindness and goodness are to help us relate to others; faithfulness, gentleness and self-control are for inner strength. The gifts of the Spirit are given in three groups: wisdom, knowledge and discerning of spirits, all necessary for leadership; faith, healing and miracles, required for helping others; prophecy, tongues and interpretation of tongues, the vocal gifts for encouragement and edification. (The Gifts of the Holy Spirit - See Notes page 98.)

Jesus makes it possible for the Holy Spirit to live in us. Our body becomes the temple of the Holy Spirit. (1 Cor. 6:15-20). The extent we allow Christ to fully possesses us is the extent to which we attain the fullness of his Spirit and his fullness is to be continually renewed. There is an ever-developing and continual growing in the life of Christ, and these baptisms are interconnected.

The fifth baptism is into the **body of Christ**, the ecclesia or church. At conversion the new believer becomes a member of the spiritual church of Jesus Christ. This church is not a denomination but the corporate spiritual "body of Christ". One cannot become a member of this church by registering on a church membership roll but by being baptized into Christ, and water baptism is the recognized Biblical manner in which one declares one's allegiance to the church of Jesus.

The word ecclesia means "chosen or called out ones" - all those who believe in and actively follow Jesus. It is the "body of Christ" on earth and comprised of young and old, male and female, Gentile and Jew, who have all been born again. It is a visible manifestation of the invisible Kingdom of God on earth. It is not the Kingdom but should reflect and declare it. The aim of the Lord is to take converts and integrate them into the spiritual body where they can grow and function, find encouragement and support, and contribute in service and mutual love and care of each other. (Rom.12:5,5, 1 Cor.12:12-27, Gal. 3:26,27, Eph. 1:22,23, 4:4,25, Phil. 1:27).

God places in this fellowship of believers, ministry gifts and we will consider them later. (1 Cor. 12:28-31).

The sixth baptism is into **suffering**.
To belong to Christ's Kingdom is to be an alien on earth and an obstacle to the kingdom of darkness. The citizens of God's Kingdom have a different world-view from that of the world and this may bring about persecution. We have already considered this as expressed by Jesus in his teaching known as the Beatitudes. The kingdoms of darkness are controlled by the devil. Many believers in numerous countries experience persecution. As we identify with each other in suffering, the church grows in maturity and blessing. Trials produce perseverance. (Luke 12:50, Mk.10:37, John 15:18, 2 Tim.3:12). We don't want this baptism but it is a reality.

I believe that there is a **seventh baptism** and although this may not be immediately apparent, I believe it is nevertheless very special. It is to know God the **Father** in an intimate relationship. As we have seen, the word baptism means to be identified with and joined to something, to be put in or made one with it. The prayer of Jesus in John 17 reveals his desire that we be one in him just as he is one in God the Father.

The Almighty God, Father, Son and Holy Spirit, is three persons in one. Jesus prayed for believers to be one in him and in the Father. (Jn. 17:11, 21-23). This is to be in perfect oneness with God and is what Jesus wants his followers to experience: to be one in the Father, the Son and the Spirit. I believe this happens in a baptism into the Father and his divine nature. Like all the other baptisms it is an ongoing experience in which we grow to know God as Father.

BAPTISM INTO THE FATHER AND HIS LOVE

This is to be one with the Father through Jesus and the Holy Spirit. To know God like this is to be baptized into his love, the love that the apostle John talks of in his epistle in which there are seventeen direct references to God's love, and many more about that love working in and through us. This entire epistle is written about how we may *know* the Father. John explains that, by knowing and abiding in God's love, it is possible to know him and be at one with him. He writes, "If we love one another, God abides in us, and His love has been made perfect in us". (1 Jn. 4:12). In this oneness we know the perfect love of "God the Father" and are able to love one another. (1 Jn. 2:13). God has lavished his love upon us so that we may be his children. (1 Jn. 3:1).

God *is* love, not that he loves, but *is* love. (1 Jn. 4:7-21, Rom. 5:5, Eph. 4:16-19, Jn. 17:26). Someone who dwells in God's love, dwells *in* God and is at one with him. His love is expressed through Jesus, for no one can come to the Father except through him. (Jn. 14:6). Jesus was sent from the Father's heart to seek the lost and bring them back to his heart. (Jn. 1:18, Luke 15:20). To truly know God is to love God and to become one with him through Christ and be a carrier of his great "agape" love. Many people are saved, know the scriptures and even do great deeds yet do not really know the Father in this way. Our aim is to love like he loves. (1 Cor. 13:1-13, Matt. 5:43-48). Love fulfills the whole law of God. (Gal. 5:14, Js. 1:25).

Some believers never seem to come to the place where they know the Father. In many churches the emphasis is only upon Jesus and in other churches it is on the Holy Spirit but God wants us to know him as

Father. Jesus is of course central and rightly so, but he wants us to know the Father. (Jn. 20:17). All his teachings were about the Father. He taught us how to pray to the Father, many of his parables are about the Father and the Father is the centre of his life and message. If we are to know God then it is to know him as our Father. It is the Father who loved us so much that he sent his Son to find us and bring us to himself. The apostle Paul wrote about it in Romans 8:14-16. Our faith is to lead us to the Father. It is important to know God as our Father through Jesus who is himself the express image of the Father. (Jn. 14:8-11, 20,21,23). As we grow in oneness with Jesus, we grow into an intimate loving relationship with God our Father. We are sanctified and loved by the Father. (Jude 1, 1 Pet. 1:14-17, 2 Cor. 6:17-7:1). We are adopted so that we can know him as Abba, our beloved Father. (Gal. 4:6).

God trains, corrects and disciplines every one of his children as a Father. (Heb. 12:5-11, Prov. 3:11,12, Rev. 3:19). He is our gardener who prunes us in order for us to grow and produce fruit. (Jn. 15). To know the Father is an incentive to a holy life. Read Matthew 6 and John 14 and count how many times Jesus talks about the Father. To know the Father, and his love, and to express it to others, is to be our spiritual goal. (1 Jn. 1:1-3). This leads into the next principle.

4 – LAYING ON OF HANDS

The fourth principle of God's Word is Fellowship and service.

This is about caring for each other in a relationship of service and <u>fellowship</u>.

Jesus often ministered to people by reaching out his hand and healing the sick, lifting them up, feeding them and so on. Our hands are the means God has given us to show love and care for others. When we meet someone, we grasp their hands, we lay hands on their shoulder or arm to comfort them, and we hug them to show joy. We express ourselves with the touch of a hand. This is not in an abusive or immoral way but in a holy manner as God's children.

Jesus ministered to bruised and broken lives by touching people with the love and power of his Father. We can do the same as his hands extended. Through touch we can help a needy person and by identify with them we become an avenue for God's divine love and power. When a person is full of the Spirit of God a simple touch can bring deliverance. Our hands are the extension of his hands through the authority that Jesus gives us. (Matt. 28:18-20).

A hand has five fingers, so the laying on of hands is used in five ways.
<u>Healing</u>: Mark 16:18, Luke 4:40,41, 13:11-13, Matt. 8:14,15.
<u>Imparting Spiritual Blessings and Gifts</u>: 1 Tim.4:14, 2 Tim. 1:6.
<u>Ordination</u>: Acts 6:6, 13:2,3, Deuteronomy 34:9, Numbers 27:18-20.
<u>For the impartation of the Holy Spirit</u>: Acts 8:17, 9:17, 19:6.
<u>Commissioning God's Missionaries</u> – Acts 15:1-3.

Laying on of hands is a means to impart God's gifts and blessings to others. Before we can give a gift, however, we must receive it from God. This is done by faith, prayer and even fasting.

This very important principle speaks of being in fellowship with others. The touch of a hand cannot be experienced in isolation and disciples of Jesus are called into fellowship and unity. The visible church is ordained by God to be the pillar and ground of truth. (1 Tim. 3:15). By "church" I do not mean a historical building but the living Spirit-filled body of Christ meeting together in fellowship and praise and prayer, Bible study, fellowship and caring for one another in communion. (Acts 2:42). The body of Christ should be structured along New Testament patterns and empowered by the Holy Spirit with prophets, evangelists, teachers and pastors functioning in apostolic teams. (Eph. 4:11). Believers are called to serve one another and the mark of a great person is their service and humility. Jesus himself set the example. (John 13:13,14). It is in this kind of fellowship that we learn to love, serve and relate to others. It is how we grow, not in isolation but wherever possible with others.

Goats are independent wild creatures found individually or in small numbers running around the hills, whereas sheep live in flocks with shepherds to guide them to green pastures. The Lord calls his followers as sheep not goats. In a flock of sheep, it is the isolated and single ones that are vulnerable to predators, and so it is with believers: the devil attacks those who are isolated. (Heb. 10:24,15). This highlights the need for having strong relationships with other believers. Members of the flock who are weak, sick, young or old should be cared for by others in the flock. This is all part of true fellowship.

5 – THE RESURRECTION OF THE DEAD – 1 Corinthians 15

The fifth principle of God's Word is the Resurrection.

Everything in our faith depends on the resurrection of Christ. (1 Cor. 15:13-17). If he did not rise then there is no hope for the future and we are all still in the grip of sin and death. However, the resurrection of Christ is an established historical fact and was witnessed by hundreds of people. Millions of people from all nations and walks of life still believe it today. (The Resurrection – See Notes page 98.)

Death is universal and because all mankind has an intrinsic fear of death many ideas about it, from reincarnation to paradise, have arisen. The cause of death is sin. (Gen. 2:17, Rom. 5:12, 6:23). The only person who is able to speak with authority on it is Jesus Christ, for he is the only person who died and came back. He was brutally tortured, sustained fatal wounds, died and was certified dead by the highest religious and secular authorities of the time. He was buried for three days before rising on the third day and then seen by hundreds of people. (Matt.12:40, 1 Cor.15:3-6). Their testimony is recorded for us. He did not appear as a disembodied spirit but in a recognizable body. After he arose, he remained on earth meeting with people, and teaching them about the Kingdom of God. He then ascended to heaven from where he will return in power and glory.

Jesus partook of death for all men and rose again and is alive today. (Heb. 2:9, Rev. 1:18). He displayed his power by raising Lazarus from the dead and he promised to raise all who believe in him. (Jn. 11:25,26, 5:21, 6:39,40,44,54). The resurrection of believers takes place at the appearing of Christ individually and collectively. (1 Cor. 15:55, 1 Thess. 4:13-18, Phil. 3:21). There is another resurrection, at the last judgment, and everyone will be in one or the other of them, either to life or to condemnation. (Rev. 20:11-15, Jn. 5:24-30).

When a believer dies the physical body dies but they immediately go in their spirit to be with the Lord. (Phil. 1:22,23). The apostle Paul described this as being "clothed" with a new immortal "house" or "body". (2 Cor. 5:1-9). In other words, they are not left disembodied spirits but are clothed with a real heavenly body. (1 Cor. 15:35-54). A funeral for a Christian is not the end and we do not sorrow as those who have no hope but are able to rejoice that they are with the Lord. (1 Thess. 4:13,14,18).

There are many testimonies of people who have "died" and been resuscitated. People have had what are called "Near Death Experiences" and amazing encounters, sometimes with angels, deceased people and even with the Lord. Many of them have been so impacted by their experience that they are no longer afraid to die. However, except for Jesus himself, no one has come back from death with a changed and immortal body. This brings us to the next principle.

6 – JUDGMENT

The sixth principle of God's Word is eternal Judgment.

There are teachers today who ignore this and believe everyone will somehow be redeemed. This teaching is called "universal salvation" and is promoted by people who believe that everyone will go to heaven. Jesus, however, did not teach this and in his final words made it clear that those who do not repent will be judged. (Rev. 21:5-8). The Bible says that God will bring all things into judgment. Because the Son of God bore the sins of all mankind, God the Father has appointed him Judge of both the living and the dead. (1 Peter 4:5). There is no one else qualified to judge except Jesus and his judgment will be fair and just. Everyone will be judged but God offers salvation to all who repent and come to him. (Heb. 9:27). This offer is made through the declaration of the Gospel which during the last 2000 years has gone to every nation. (Lk. 24:36,37). God has raised up many devoted people to declare the Gospel worldwide. However, there are people throughout the ages who have not heard or had the opportunity to believe and receive salvation. God will not condemn anyone who has not had a proper opportunity to receive his mercy. I believe everyone will in some way be given an opportunity at some time to hear and receive forgiveness, mercy and eternal life. (Rom. 2:14-16). Only if that offer is rejected will condemnation take place.

God's promise is that "whoever believes in Jesus should not perish but have everlasting life". (Jn. 3:16,17). God is a God of justice in all things. (1 Jn. 1:9, Rev. 15:3) Righteousness and justice are the foundation of His throne. (Ps. 89.14). Jesus is the Saviour of all who trust in him. Believers will stand before the judgment "seat of Christ" not in condemnation but in grace and forgiveness. All who repent and receive him pass from condemnation to life. (2 Cor. 5:9,10, Rom. 14:10-12).

The kingdom of darkness and all who serve in it will, from the devil down be destroyed. (Matt. 13:40, Jude 14,15, 2 Thess.1:7-9, Rev. 20:10). God's mercy is extended to all through Christ, the just for the unjust, but people who knowingly reject God's mercy forfeit it by their own choice. (1 Pet. 3:18) Outside of Christ there is no forgiveness. It is necessary for men and women to repent and receive Christ now while they are able to do so. One day every individual will bow before him. (Ps. 22:29, Phil. 2:10).

ETERNAL JUDGMENT

Judgment will be eternal in its outcome. All mankind is heading for an eternal destiny, either with God or without God. To be with God in heaven is to be in a place of blessing beyond all ability to comprehend. (1 Cor. 2:9). It is a real place in which there is no suffering of any kind. There is no pain, death or sickness in the new heaven and earth and New Jerusalem, the city of God is beautiful and majestic beyond all description. (Rev. 21:4, 22:1-5). It is full abundant *eternal* life.

To be with God in heaven will be truly wonderful. To be separated from God, however, is to suffer *eternal* death. There are different understandings among Christians as to what this means, some think it is eternal suffering, others that it is total annihilation. Either way it should be taken very seriously and people should consider their eternal destination. (Rev. 21:8). We ourselves choose where we will go.

The destiny of Satan, and all who reject God, is total, irrevocable, destruction and loss. Their own decision will bring this upon them. (Jn. 3:16,17). (See Edward Fudge - Notes page 98).

7 – GROWING UP IN CHRIST – Going on to maturity - Heb.6:1

The seventh principle of God's Word is to keep going on to perfection and maturity. The word maturity means "to be a finisher, to complete what is started". It is the principle of "growing in faith to attain Christ's perfection". We are to grow in him and allow him to grow in us so that we reach spiritual maturity in him. The idea that a believer is immediately mature and perfect is false; believers need to grow into the fullness of God's purposes for them. From the moment a person receives Christ, they pass out of death into life and are called out of the world and its values and set apart for heaven. This new life is not just for the future but begins immediately. Christ will one day present his church perfect, but until then his command is to "seek first the Kingdom of God" and for us to press into it with determination. (Matt. 6:33, 11:12). He came to give us life and life more abundantly. (Jn. 10:10).

There is a wonderful old hymn – *"I have decided to follow Jesus (x3), no turning back, no turning back"*. Jesus called his disciples to follow him as their shepherd. As our shepherd he will guide us through life and bring us to our heavenly destiny. (Ps. 23).

The life of a believer is one of pressing through every test, trial, setback and difficulty to win the high calling of Christ. (Phil. 3:7-16). Believers are not expected to sit back and do nothing but to mature in faith in Christ. The word "mature" used in the NIV Bible also means to be *perfected* but we will only be perfect when we see Jesus face to face and are changed. Until then we are being changed spiritually into his image. We are "perfect" to the measure of maturity that we have attained in Christ. We grow deeper in understanding as we grow, and are changed bit by bit. (1 Cor. 13:10,11, 14:20). This is an ongoing process and we are to go on, going on. The words *perfect* and *mature* also mean in the Bible "to be a finisher", to complete what God has started.

By understanding and practicing these seven principles it is possible to "go on to maturity". Each principle is linked with and proceeds from the others. Through repentance a believer is forgiven and delivered from sin, reborn by the Spirit of God and adopted into God's family, separated from the world and through faith brought into a daily walk with God, which leads to caring for people, serving others and becoming fruitful in service. As we learn and practice the principles of God's Word we continue to grow spiritually and are changed from glory to glory. (2 Cor.3:18).

The early church devoted themselves to doing four things: the teaching of the apostles, prayers, fellowship and breaking of bread. In this way they grew spiritually. (Acts 2:42).

BUILDING OUR LIVES ON CHRIST THE ROCK

In Matthew chapters 5 to 7 Jesus instructed the crowds that followed him about the principles for living a life that would be of eternal worth, and he summed it up with a parable about a man who built his house upon a rock. (Matt. 7:24-27). The meaning of the parable is clear: Christ is the Rock and we should build our lives upon him and his words. Those who do so will survive the storms of life. Jesus Christ is the "Rock of Ages" and never changes. He is the eternal Lord and is the same yesterday, today and forever. (Heb. 13:8, 1:10-12).

To live a life of faith we need to put these principles into action.

MATH 16:18

CHAPTER 6 –TWO KINGDOMS AT WAR

At the crucifixion two kingdoms clashed. Jesus did not come as a king with an army, but as a servant. In the guise of a carpenter from Nazareth he was in fact the holy Son of God, yet also a man having being born of a woman. Satan sought to destroy him. The King of heaven was put on trial. He stood before the most powerful earthly authorities of the time, both secular and spiritual. A battle for the hearts of men raged that day. Some despised him despite the miracles he had done and they falsely accused him, mocked him, rejected him and crucified him. Others wept for him. As he hung on the cross the sun turned dark and would not shine and darkness enveloped the land. Christ proved too pure for evil to overcome him. He died and rose again on the third day. But it was Satan who put him there.

The clash between light and darkness still rages in the *hearts* of men and women everywhere. The way we live will either draw us to the cross or repel us away from it. We are all part of this spiritual conflict and until we make Christ Lord in our hearts, we will never have peace.

THE BATTLE IN THE HEARTS OF MEN – SPIRITUAL WARFARE

A battle still rages within people today. Each person has a choice, to either reject the love of God and give allegiance to the kingdom of darkness, or to yield to Christ and enter his Kingdom. Within each heart there is a battlefield and a throne. Whoever sits on the throne decides the outcome of the battle. If we dethrone self and crown Christ as King of our lives, we will be delivered from the kingdom of darkness and become part of Christ's Kingdom. This is what the thief who died beside Jesus did. He saw through the accusations and recognized Jesus as the true King. He cried out, "Lord, remember me when you come into your Kingdom" and immediately got the assurance that he needed. The other thief refused. (Luke 23:39-43). This illustrates the two pathways from which we must choose. There is no middle road. There is a war within our souls; two opposing kingdoms clash within us. (Gal. 5:17, Rom. 8:6-8, 1 Peter 2:11). Satan has enslaved the world and blinds the spiritual eyes of many people. (Eph. 4:17,18). There is no light in them and darkness rules them. (Matt. 6:22). However, when Christ's light shines into hearts it dispels the darkness. This process continues as the believer grows in Christ, for when Jesus comes in, he brings his light with him. (1 John 2:8-11).

BODY, SOUL and SPIRIT   *[handwritten: Personel warfare]*

We are comprised of Body, Soul and Spirit. (Heb. 4:12, 1 Thess. 5:23). Our spirit is God-conscious, our soul is self-conscious, and our body is world-conscious. The *soul* of man is his personality, his heart and mind - his person. The *spirit* of man is that which animates and influences him, his deep inner thoughts and will. One can have a timid and fearful spirit, or a bold and fearless spirit. The spirit has access to the mind and can control feelings and motives. The *body* is the vessel in which both soul and spirit live and is linked with the passions and emotions seated in the soul. Since the fall, men and women have a "carnal" nature which is the worldly, sinful nature of natural man. (Gal. 5:19, Rom. 8:5,6:6, 1 Cor.2:14, Js. 3:14-16). The spiritual and carnal natures are constantly interacting in the soul. Until born again people live under the law of sin which produces death, but through Christ we can live in the law of the Spirit which gives life. (Rom. 8:2).

God made Adam a spiritual being dwelling in a physical body. Adam's spirit governed both his soul and body but this order was reversed when he fell. Temptation came in through the eyes; Eve saw that the forbidden fruit was good and "pleasant in her eyes". She ignored the Word of God and believed the forbidden fruit would make her wise, and she ate it. She was deceived, through believing a lie and doubting God. Sin entered through the flesh, the mind and soul was deceived, and the spirit suffered a death blow. Sin brought death.

Note the progressive direction of Satan's deception – through the eyes (her body), into her mind (become wise), and on to her spirit (become like God). (Gen. 3:1-7). Note that Satan tempted Christ in a similar way: to turn stones into bread - *physical* hunger; receive adulation - self-exultation, *soul*; the worship of Satan, *spiritual* deception.

Satan seeks to captivate us body, soul and spirit. The Bible talks of the <u>outer</u> man, the joints and marrow of the body, and the <u>*inner*</u> man, the thoughts and intents of the soul and spirit. (Heb. 4:12, 2 Cor .4:16, Eph. 3:16) There is nothing evil in the physical body: it is a marvel of creation, but after the fall the "carnal nature" became the seat of sin. God wants to sanctify us in spirit, soul and body and when we identify with Jesus this sinful nature is "crucified with Christ". (1 Thess. 5:23, Gal. 2:20, Rom. 6:6-14). He took our sinful nature and died with it. He put it to death and then rose for us in his sinlessness. This was possible because as the Son of Man he was put to death in his body for our sins, and then because he is the perfect sinless Son of God he arose in his eternal Spirit. (1 Pet. 3:18, 1 Cor. 15:45). When we receive Jesus, he is able to come into us by his Spirit and join with our spirit and give us new life. We are joined to him and benefit from all that he did. We are "put into" him and he comes into us. This is the rebirth. *That which is born of the flesh is flesh that which is born of the spirit is spirit.* (John 3:6). To receive salvation, you must be born through the Spirit of Jesus, God's holy Son. (Gal. 4:6).

PRINCIPLES TO DEVELOP THE NEW LIFE

The Holy Spirit then works in us to produce the nature of Christ. Depending on whether we sow to the spirit or to the flesh, we will reap the benefits or consequences. If we feed the carnal nature with its selfish desires, the inevitable result will be "works of the flesh". (Gal. 5:19-22). Whichever life is fed will grow stronger. If we cultivate the "spiritual man" and mortify the "old man" we will bear spiritual fruit.

THE "PUTTING ON AND PUTTING OFF" PRINCIPLE

By repenting and receiving Christ a person *dies* to sin and their spirit becomes *alive* to God. They are born again and live as a *new creation* the life of Christ, turning from the *old* dead self. (2 Cor. 5:17). This becomes a principle to live by, described as "putting on the new and putting off the old". (Col. 3:8-14, Eph. 4:22-31). It is a process whereby the old nature, having received a death-blow, is mortified and dies. As we have seen, the fallen nature is *buried* with Christ: now we must *reckon* ourselves to be dead to it. (Rom. 6:4-11). This applies to our old nature which God now considers dead when Christ died. When he died, he did so *in our place*; he did what we could not do, took our sins, paid in full the penalty for them, died and rose again for us. Not only are our sins buried with him but our entire sinful nature is dead and buried with him and we have a new nature. That is the way God now sees us, free of sin.

The devil, however, is a persistent deceiver and does all he can to keep resurrecting our "old nature". He gets at us by trying to revive our fallen flesh nature. He keeps working on our weaknesses, tripping us up with failings, and shortfalls. He is a counterfeit worker of false miracles and tries to resurrect the "old life". He endeavors to revive areas within us such as self-pity, fear and rejection, if we have not fully repented from them. He will throw temptations at us such as bad literature, bad company, bad thoughts, and other things. He tries to persuade us to yield to wrong desires and selfish motives. By doing this, believers can be misled if they don't put off the old and put on the new. (2 Cor. 7:1). It is like breathing, we let out old air and breathe in new air, so too we take in the new life of Christ and dispel the old life of sin. Its like going to the loo, we eat good food and dump the waste.

Christians are not immune from demonic attack and although being "new creations" may still need deliverance. They have been forgiven but may not be fully living in the new life. On occasion, through lack of discipleship or proper instruction, or a great weakness on their part, Satan can cause defeat and bondage. Temptation is the work of the devil and can result in demonic bondage within the person, which can then affect them in their body, soul and spirit.

Through the ages a fierce conflict has raged in the world and in the hearts of men and women. It will continue until Jesus returns. We are in this conflict and can experience victory: Christ is able to deliver us from evil. There are ways to counteract the attacks and have a full and meaningful spiritual walk and abundant life in Christ. It is through obedience that victory comes. Many nominal Christians want Christ to be Saviour but have not yielded to his total Lordship in their lives.

We are told to "put on Christ" and be clothed with him. (Gal. 3:27, Rom. 13:12-14, Eph. 4:24). When his life dwells in us, peace, power and victory prevail. He shines within us and dispels darkness and changes us from glory to glory. (2 Cor. 3:18, Prov. 4:18,19). By dying to self and living to Christ we are delivered from every stronghold. This is the work of faith. Just as we put on clothes to cover ourselves, so too we "put on" Christ. He is our covering and protection. We are not defenseless but have an "armour". (Eph. 6:11). As soldiers we are called to "fight the good fight of faith" and as every soldier must undergo training in warfare so we must too. Every believer is involved in some way. This "putting on putting off" principle reaches it fullness when we put off our physical body at death and rise in our spirit body.

THE DEVIL IS REAL

It is a sign of the times in which we live that many people don't believe either in God or the devil. The consequence of this is evident in the terrible state of society and the world. Just as each person can trust in a personal Saviour if they so choose, so too whether they admit it or not, every person has a personal enemy and can come under attack. Evil is not just an influence but originates from a powerful spiritual being, and the whole world lies under his sway. (1 Jn. 5:19). Each person has a personal malicious enemy who hates them and will do everything to hurt and destroy them. If you do not admit this you will be unable to resist him or escape him.

Jesus was also personally attacked and confronted by Satan when he was on earth. (Matt. 4:1-11). This was not a philosophical experience but a real encounter. Jesus did not have dark thoughts of his own but he was tempted and attacked directly by the devil. He battled against the most powerful spiritual being there is, outside of God, and he used the Word of God for his defense. So must we. The devil can afflict us with all manner of things and we must learn to use God's Word just as Jesus did. In order to do this, we must read his Word. We are to let "the Word of Christ dwell in us richly". (Col. 3:16). His Word is more important than anything else. If watching TV, going to sports functions, or anything else takes priority over reading the Word then we will not be able to withstand the enemy. We must not be conformed to this world's ways but transformed by the renewing of our mind. (Rom. 12: 3-6). This is a process in which we are actively involved. The apostle Paul said that "the weapons of our warfare are mighty to the pulling down of every stronghold and argument against Christ and to bring every thought captive to him". (2 Cor. 10:3-5).

We must stop listening to "devil-talk" and listen to God-talk. Often people speak to themselves and even reply to themselves and sadly listen to all the negative things they say about themselves. By debasing themselves with words of self-condemnation they do the devil's work for him. We are to talk to the Lord and listen to what *he* says to us. To do this we have to read his Word and give the Lord time to speak through it. Communion is dialogue, not monologue. Jesus illustrated this by telling of a man who prayed "with himself". (Matt. 18:11 AMP). That is not prayer but pretense!

In his letter to the Ephesians Paul wrote that we were all once held by the mind of the flesh. (Eph. 2:3). He went on to say that we should no longer walk in the futility of that mind but should put off the former way of thinking and be renewed in the spirit of our mind which is created according to true righteousness. (Eph. 4:17-24). He goes on to instruct us how to put on the <u>whole armour of God</u>.

THE ARMOUR OF GOD - Ephesians 6:10-20

When we become believers in Christ, we become involved in a war between two kingdoms. In this conflict we have spiritual armor to help us. This armour is especially provided for us so that we can overcome every battle we personally face in our lives and circumstances. We are told therefore to put on the armour of God and to make a stand.

Christ has authority over all the power of darkness. He smashed the kingdom of darkness and its demonic deception. (Matt. 12:28,29). Just as Abraham was called to live by faith in the "promised land", so we too are called to do so figuratively. Just as his progeny were delivered from Egypt where they had become slaves and entered the "promised land", so believers too must leave the old life of sin and learn to live in the "land of faith". There are giants there, it is true, but they are defeated through Jesus. Just as David slew Goliath, so we can defeat the giants we face. David trusted in the Lord and was able to defeat Goliath by using a sling and a pebble. So too we have been given the means through faith and the Word of God to defeat the giants we face.

We have already considered the putting on/putting off principle. Now we are told to put on the whole armour of God. There are seven vital things the armour gives us which illustrate seven ways we can defend ourselves from the "wiles of the devil". Here is a brief list of them.

First, we are to put on the "belt of truth". Soldiers at that time wore a short skirt secured by a strong girdle, or belt, which supported the muscles of the waist and strengthened the entire body. Truth is like a belt and a fundamental necessity above all else. There is one thing the devil cannot stand against and that is truth. Jesus Christ is not a truth but "the Truth". (Jn. 1:14,17, 5:33, 8:32, 14:6,17, 16:13, 17:17, 1 Thess. 2:13, 2 Tim. 2:15). Truth is not a subjective notion, so prevalent in today's philosophies, but is the uncompromising unchanging truth found in Jesus Christ as declared in his Word. His Words will never pass away. (Matt. 24:35). We are to apply them in all our actions and decisions: we should never resort to hypocrisy or dishonesty. God honours truth, the devil fears and despises it. We must stand for truth.

Second, we are to put on the breastplate of righteousness. This breastplate covers and guards our heart. Notice it is not putting on our own righteousness but God's. We have no righteousness of our own but rely wholly upon Christ's. (Rom. 3:10, Isa. 64:6). Any righteousness we may have accrued is through the merit of Christ who declares us to be righteous. He did a swap with us, he took our "rags of righteousness" and replaced them with the righteousness of God. (2 Cor. 5:21). For believers, righteousness is imparted not earned. By our faith in him Christ accredits us with his own righteousness. (Rom. 3:10, 21-25, Tit. 3:4-8). He gives us a credit note to say that we are righteous. (Gal. 2:16). *God himself justifies us and declares us to be righteous in his sight.* We display his righteousness not our own. When it says that we put on the breastplate of righteousness, it is not our breastplate but Christ's. By doing this we exalt Christ, affirm our trust in him and safeguard our own actions, for it is impossible to deliberately do anything unrighteous while wearing his breastplate, and any "works of righteousness" that we do are the result of Christ's righteousness in us not our own. (2 Cor. 5:21). Righteousness is taken out of self-effort and placed wholly in Christ. He alone is righteous. The breastplate is one of faith and do this in faith. (1 Thess. 5:8).

Once we put it on Satan can no longer tempt us, for we are protected by Christ. We are to live a life of righteousness, but this is not trying to earn salvation or prove how good we are, and if we do fall the Holy Spirit convicts us and we confess our sin and are cleansed. (1 John 1:9). Satan is called the "accuser of the brethren" and our defense is to affirm that we have Christ's righteousness. We are heirs of righteousness, just as Noah was, and also Abraham, and multitudes of others through the ages. (Jas. 2:23, Heb. 11:2). None of these people were perfect, but they all trusted in God.

Satan can't get to us if we are *in* Christ. Christ has defeated him. So, we are hidden in Christ, we are in him and he is our champion, our strength and victory. Lots of believers fall into the trap of relying upon their own righteousness but that fails. Instead we stand clothed in Christ's righteousness.

Third, we are to put on the shoes of the Gospel of peace. Shoes are essential, especially for soldiers. They must be strong and have a firm grip so that we stand and don't slip or fall. Our feet are in regular contact with the earth and carry us everywhere. If our feet are shod with the Gospel of Peace then we carry it everywhere and are able to walk in peace and stand firm in every situation. To stand firm is vital in life. There is a saying: "If you don't stand for something you will fall for anything". If you are sure about what you believe in you will not be moved from it. The "Gospel of Peace" is what the world needs and the foundation on which we stand is Jesus our rock of salvation. This is why the *preparation* of the Gospel is important. It is our readiness to both live by the Gospel and also to share it. If our lives are grounded in the Gospel of Peace we are protected from the world's strife and have peace. It gives us peace in a troubled world afflicted with uncertainty. The Gospel brings peace not war.

Jesus said that we should be "peacemakers". (Matt. 5:9). Not peace keepers but peacemakers. The Gospel *makes* peace, peace with God and peace with one another. This is not the peace of compromise but the peace which comes with truth. It brings peace in trouble, despair and hopelessness. It is sown in peace and brings a harvest of righteousness and fruits of peace. (Js. 3:17,18). Those who believe the Gospel have the "peace of God that passes all understanding". (Phil. 4:6,7). If you don't have peace, for instance about something you are thinking or doing, then it may mean you are not in God's perfect will or may be in disobedience and need to repent and stop doing it. If on the other hand you have no peace about something that is out of your control you can come to God in prayer and give it to him and receive perfect peace. The world needs to receive the Gospel of peace. "How beautiful are the feet of those who preach the gospel of peace, who bring glad tidings of good things". (Rom. 10:14,15). Notice that it is the "preparation" of the Gospel that is necessary. We put these shoes on in order to walk in peace and to share the Gospel with others. We can all share God's peace and be peacemakers in a needy world.

<u>Fourth, we are to take the shield of faith.</u> The first three items are all part of a soldier's regular "clothing". We are now instructed about three more items which are necessary in a conflict. The first is a <u>shield</u> and is absolutely vital for every soldier to have for personal protection. A shield is not offensive but defensive. The larger the shield, the more protection it affords and so too we must grow in faith to appropriate the promises of God. (2 Pet. 1:1-3). The large Roman shields were rectangular and could form a covering for a whole contingent of soldiers which nothing could penetrate. So too our faith can protect us individually and collectively from the wiles of the enemy. (Eph.6:11).

We have already considered some aspects of faith and this "shield of faith" is an extra bulwark against the fiery darts the enemy may use to attack us personally.

Some thoughts we have can actually originate from the adversary who may bombard us with all manner of accusations, temptations and lies. As already said, the devil is the "accuser of the brethren" and, just as he attacked Jesus, so he can attack us. He can bombard us with bad thoughts and attempt to influence our motives and desires. Sometimes we may also suffer verbal attacks from people, workmates and even family and it may be that adverse circumstances are at times engineered against us so that we require the shield of faith for our protection. (Ps. 140:3). When we call to the Lord, he is able to give us immediate encouragement from scripture and from his Spirit which. The Lord himself is our great protector, as he said to Abram, "I am your shield". (Gen. 15:1).

Fifth, we are to take the helmet of salvation. This helmet is to protect our minds with the assurance of salvation, which is the confidence we need in order to face upheavals in life and the difficulties we may face individually and in the world. (1 Thess.5:8). It is this assurance that gives us security and enables us to be more than conquerors. We can say, no matter what, "It is well with my soul": the final outcome is certain. (Rom. 8:37).

There are some Christians who are never sure whether they are saved or not. They argue from certain scriptures that one can have no assurance about salvation and must continually strive to be saved, as if it is up to us to somehow attain it. These believers are, in my mind, unbelievers, or else they have never understood the truth about the salvation God wrought in Jesus. He said of those who follow him, "they shall never perish, neither shall any man pluck them out of my hand". (Jn. 10:28,29). Our salvation is not dependent on ourselves but on him. It is a gift and is a sure and certain hope. (1 Thess.5:9). It is not a vain hope but a *sure* hope. (Heb. 6:17-20). The devil will try everything possible to shake our confidence in Christ but his promise is steadfast and we are anchored to God who cannot lie. Jesus is the author of eternal salvation to all who obey him. (Heb. 5:9). Our salvation is not dependent on us but on him. What Christ has done can never be undone. The devil can never change it. What we must do is believe it. There are so many promises that affirm our salvation once a resolute commitment to Christ has been made, and it would require another book to contain them all. It is true that some people make a false start and never carry on but the mark of true repentance, as we have said, is to keep going on.

As we read and believe God's Word his salvation protects our minds against every vain thing the enemy will throw at us, every test and trial, every disappointment and sorrow. The problem many people have is that they don't read God's Word and they don't believe it. God says he will put his laws in our minds and write them on our hearts. (Heb. 8:10,11). They are not written on stone but on our hearts and minds, and the more we read God's Word the more of a sound mind is given to us until we have the mind of Christ and can truly say that we know him. "Let this mind be in you that was in Christ". (Titus 1:7, Phil.2:5).

Sixth, we are to take the Sword of the Spirit which is the Word of God. This is the only piece of the armour that is offensive: all the others are defensive. The Roman sword was a short dagger used in hand-to-hand combat and needed for personal conflict with the enemy. Notice this spiritual sword is God's Word not our own. It is God's Word that we use against the enemy. It has nothing to do with our own strength or ability but everything to do with God's. God's authority and power is found in his Word; not in rebuking or decreeing or binding but in using the Word of God as a skilled soldier uses a sword. We are therefore to know his Word and use it as Jesus did. When Satan attacked him by misquoting scripture, Jesus spoke the correct Word straight back at him. (Matt. 4:4).

The original Greek word used for God's spoken Word is *Rhema,* and it is when God's Word is spoken with the authority and anointing of the Holy Spirit. There is nothing more powerful than speaking aloud God's Word. (Rom. 10:8, 1 Pet. 1:25).

I would encourage people not to speak to the devil with their own words but to use God's Word to rebuff him. There is no instruction in scripture to speak to the devil on our own initiative: our defense is

God's Word which is powerful even to the thoughts and intents of the heart. (Heb. 4:12).

Seventh, we are to pray in the Spirit. It is no good putting on the armour unless we also pray. Praying in the Spirit is not praying by rote or repetition but with prayers that are inspired and energized by the Spirit of God. Jesus taught us how to pray and we will have more to say about this later. I believe that "praying in the Spirit" includes the gift of speaking in an unknown language as the Holy Spirit gives the ability to do so. This is a very powerful way to pray under the control of God's Spirit. (1 Cor.14:15). We will consider more later.

WHAT IS "SPIRITUAL WARFARE"

God's armour is given to us because we fight not against flesh and blood but are involved in a spiritual war. (Eph. 6:11,12). Satan has legions of demons that do his bidding and are in rebellion against God. They look for ways to attack and hinder God's people, and at times we must wrestle against them. This can be a very personal conflict, but they must submit to the authority of Christ's Word which we can use together with God's armour. (Mark 16:17,18, Luke 10:17).

There are different levels in prayer, such as requesting, interceding, petitioning, all of which carry the meaning of us coming in humility and faith to God and asking him to supply our need. (1 Tim.2:1). Another level of prayer is intercession, which is to plead for another or even for a nation and can involve great sacrifice. Moses, Ester and Daniel did this. (Ex.32:32, Ps.106:23, Est.4:16). It was Jesus who ultimately interceded for us and paid the supreme price with his life.

The pronouncing of decrees is now a popular practice and is done with the intention of announcing God's purposes over people and nations. This has become common in some circles and can involve "declaring, decreeing, binding, rebuking, pulling down of strongholds and disarming spiritual powers. This has replaced the customary method of prayer. The direction is reversed; instead of people coming to God in humility and need, they come as kings with decrees. Declaring one's faith is one thing but decreeing things into existence is not Biblical. It comes from the false practice of naming and claiming.

Declaring and affirming God's Word in our own lives is very powerful but we must be cautious about using scripture to make all sorts of decrees. We cannot just quote things and decree them out of context to what they apply. For example, to use God's Word to decree blessing over people or whole nations that are not serving him but walking in rebellion against him, is to misuse God's Word. God will not bless unbelievers unless they repent, and his promise to those in rebellion is judgment not blessing. We must be careful in the way we handle God's Word. (Isa.66:1-6). The mark of false prophets is that they continually misappropriate and misapply it.

I hear people rebuking the devil in prayer and do not encourage this practice. We are told to *resist* the devil, not to rebuke him. (1 Pet. 5:9, Js. 4:7). To resist means to withstand him. Individual demonic activity, oppression and possession by demonic spirits, can be dealt with by commanding the spirits to depart. However, even though the Lord gave the disciples authority over demons, there is no injunction for us to rebuke Satan: quite the contrary, even the archangel did not bring accusations against him. (Jude 8,9, 2 Pet. 2:9-11). Jesus dealt with every attack from Satan by using the "Word of God" and we can too, by standing on the scriptures. Satan cannot argue with that. It is not wise to pray to the Lord in one breath and speak to the devil in the next. We pray to the Lord, and resist the devil through scripture. In this way we keep ourselves protected. The preaching of the Gospel is what brings deliverance to people and nations, not decreeing or rebuking. People must hear and repent. If there is demonic resistance or manifestations of various kinds, we have authority to correct it and by defeating demons here on earth Satan's kingdom falls in the heavens. (Lk. 11:18).

When it comes to praying for a particular community or nation, we are to operate in the manner Daniel and other great men and women prayed. Their intercession was based on *confession* and *repentance.* (Dan. 9:3-21). When Daniel prayed during a twenty-one day fast, a powerful angel broke through the spiritual strongholds and, as a result of his prayers, got the upper hand. (Dan. 10:2-19). This angel was involved in an angelic battle but Daniel did not rebuke any angels but prayed confession and repentance. There is a battle in the heavenly realms among angels and there is a battle on earth among men and demons and we must not mix the two. The principle of intercession is not rebuking, decreeing or declaring but repentance and confession. As a result, God's angels are empowered to gain victory in their realm. Our prayers of confession enable them to be victorious in battle. We must do what angels cannot do and that is to offer prayers of repentance. This breaks Satan's power. There is a scripture, 2 Chr.7:13,14, that highlights the principle of confession, repentance. There is one thing the devil cannot resist and that is truth expressed in confession, repentance and obedience to God. That defeats him.

There are multitudes of angels that protect God's people. (Ps.34:7, 91:11,12, 2 Kings 6:17). We do not pray to them, but we walk in God's protection and when we need them, they minister to us. (Heb.1:14).

TWO PRINCIPLES – THE LAW OF SIN AND DEATH and THE LAW OF THE SPIRIT OF LIFE

The law God gave Moses was never intended to give eternal life but to give instruction on conduct and bring repentance when broken. The Lord knew that it was impossible for fallen mankind to keep it. It was never intended to replace faith. The people, however, got the idea that if they kept God's laws, they would eventually become righteous. Over a period of time a mentality took hold among the spiritual leaders that culminated in what became known as the "righteousness of the Pharisees", who considered themselves to be righteous by the "works of the law". It is depicted in the story Jesus told of two men and their different attitudes. (Lk. 18:10-14).

The apostle Paul corrected this falsehood in his epistle to the Romans. In chapter 7 the "law" is mentioned over twenty times. Paul explained that the "law of sin and death" makes it impossible, in our own strength, to keep God's Law for it produces only condemnation and death. He cried out "who can deliver me from this body of death?" (Rom. 7:24).

In chapter 8:2 he gave the answer and spoke of another law, the "law of the Spirit of life in Christ" which delivers us from condemnation and enables us to walk in the Spirit not the flesh. (Rom. 8:1-8). The answer is in turning away from our self-motivated attempts to keep the law and to live in the Spirit of Jesus and thereby receive divine ability to walk in his life. He explained that those who have received the Spirit of Christ and live in his Spirit are free from the law of sin and death.

This supernatural life is only possible through the power of the risen Christ. (Rom. 8:9-11). By trusting wholly in Christ and drawing from his Spirit, we put to death the deeds of the body, and the power of the law of death is cancelled. Instead we experience the liberty of being children and not slaves. (Rom. 8:12-17). We are children of God through Jesus, the Son of God. As expressed earlier, it is God's will that we should know him as our Father. He has adopted us as sons and daughters and we can have a loving and close relationship with him as our Father. (Gal. 4:4-7). This means our status is one of heirs in the Kingdom of God.

Paul wrote the most amazing truths about living in the Spirit of Christ. (Rom. 8:18-30). He explained how the Spirit of God makes intercession for us, so that everything works together for our good. We are no longer under condemnation. Christ makes intercession for us and God himself foreknew us, predestined us, justified us and will also glorify us. (Rom. 8:31-39). Paul concludes by saying that nothing can separate us from the love of God. This is the one truth above all others that enables us to endure all things and to overcome through Christ. It is these astonishing, stupendous truths that make us more than conquerors through him who loved us.

THE RICHES OF HIS GRACE

All this is accomplished by God's grace and mercy towards us. (Eph. 1:7-10, 1 Tim.1:2, 2 Tim.1:2, Tit.1:4, 3:5, Heb.4:14-16, 1 Pet. 1:1-5).

The meaning of the Biblical word grace is so great that it is hard to fully define. It includes generosity, favour, loving-kindness, goodness, blessing, benefit, joy and unlimited abundance - and is used to describe the divine influence of God, working in the hearts of men and women to receive that which they are not worthy of having and cannot attain by their own efforts. It means we can receive what we do not deserve. Mercy is to *not* receive what we deserve, which is judgment.

"There is a great difference between Adam's sin and God's gracious gift. For the sin of this one man, Adam, brought death to many. But even greater is God's wonderful grace and his gift of forgiveness to many through this other man Jesus Christ. And the result of God's gracious gift is very different from the result of that one man's sin. For Adam's sin led to condemnation but God's free gift leads to our being made right with God, even though we are guilty of many sins. For the sin of this one man, Adam, caused death to rule over many. But even greater is God's wonderful grace and his gift of righteousness, for all who receive it will live in triumph over sin and death through this one man, Jesus Christ." – Rom. 5:15-17 NLT.

God's grace is one of the great truths in the Bible and it is given through Jesus Christ and him alone. (Jn. 1:14-17). It is *his* grace that sets us free from the bondage of sin. (Rom. 5:18-21, 6:1,2).

There is a false teaching that it is not serious for believers to continue in sin, because grace covers all their sins. Paul discounted this idea and said believers are to *reckon* themselves dead to sin and not allow it to reign in their mortal bodies. The very reason that believers have been set free from the condemnation of sin is in order to live *holy* lives and to continue to grow in God's grace. (Rom. 6:5-22). We are not under the law of sin and death but under the gift of grace and life.

"WORKS OF THE FLESH" AND "FRUITS OF THE SPIRIT"

The principle of growing in Jesus requires us to feed our spiritual nature and thereby produce spiritual fruit. Fruit does not appear on a plant immediately but requires favorable climate, nurturing and maturing as well as prevention from harmful pests. In spiritual terms this means several things: feeding on the Word of God, seeking godly fellowship and staying away from harmful influences and destructive forces that are not helpful or conducive to a life of faith. We are called away from things that are in opposition to God's Kingdom. As we have seen, there are two kingdoms and no one can live in them both at the same time. A man called Lot tried to do so and lost everything. You can read his story in Genesis chapter 19. <u>Compromise</u> with the world, its standards and values, is one of the biggest hindrances preventing people from living a life of faith.

This world is under judgment and believers are called "to come out from it and be separate", and thereby not come under its judgment but be set apart to God. Believers are to keep themselves from the world and no longer live as unbelievers. (1 Pet. 4:1-4). We are in the world but not of it. The Bible says that friendship with the world is enmity with God. "Do not love the world or the things of the world. If anyone loves the world, the love of the Father is not in him". (1 Jn. 1:15-17).

The "<u>fruits of the Spirit</u>" are in contrast to the "<u>works of the flesh</u>" listed in Galatians 5:16-25 and Ephesians 5:2-13. The works of the flesh are not just "big sins" like murder but things like carousing, arguing, crude language, revelry, and so on. We can be exposed to them through TV, bad magazines, coarse movies, bad company, bad habits, swearing and so on. They affect the way people think, act and talk, with criticism, cursing, foul speech, lying, vile jokes, accusations etc. It is our responsibility to steer away from these things. (2 Pet. 2:18-22). We cannot shut ourselves away in a sterile environment or monastery but we are able through "the divine nature to escape the corruption that is in the world". (2 Pet. 1:4). We are able to influence others if we live a different lifestyle but if we are like the world our words will carry no weight. Our tongue *defines* us and if uncontrolled *defiles* our whole body. (Js. 3:2-12). To speak badly grieves the Holy Spirit of God and such talk should be "put off". (Eph. 4:30). Jesus said that people are identified by their fruit. Our words will either justify or condemn us. (Matt. 7:16-20, 12:33-37). We need to be obedient to the Holy Spirit and allow him to correct what we say and do. He lives in us and when we violate his nature, we will feel his grief. This brings us correction or, as the Bible says, "chastening". (Heb. 12:8-11). We will either feed the "old nature" or feed the "new nature" and whichever we feed will grow stronger.

When Jesus returns the kingdom of light and the kingdom of darkness will be entirely separated. (Matt. 25:32). We cannot be in both.

We are called to a life of holiness. Believers are instructed to *"Come out from among them and be separate, says the Lord. Do not touch what is unclean, and I will receive you."*. (2 Cor. 6:14-18,7:1). The need to be sanctified is expressed in a powerful way through the imagery of Christ as the bridegroom of the church his bride. (Eph. 5:26,27). The true church is holy and without blemish. Holiness doesn't just happen but comes about through a life consecrated to God, set apart for Christ, and separate from the values of the world. Holiness is not the gift of righteousness that we receive through faith in Christ but the work of sanctification that is wrought in us as we yield our lives fully to God. We are called out of this world's value systems to walk with the Lord. Righteousness is a gift, whereas holiness is a work in us through obedience. It is God's intention for his church to be holy and, one day, he will present as a pure bride. (Rev. 19:7-9).

Our aim therefore is to be holy, even as he is holy. (Eph. 1:4, 2:21, Col. 1:22, 3:12, 1 Pet. 1:13-16). It is a process that involves tests, trials, and endurance. It is allowing the Spirit of God, through surrender and obedience, to develop the nature and image of Christ within us. As he does so the fruits of God's Spirit grow in us and we are changed. (2 Cor. 3:17,18). The result is "sanctification". (1 Pet. 1:2, 1 Thess. 5:23).

The fruits of a holy life are listed in Galatians as love, joy, peace and other wonderful characteristics of a life yielded to God. (Gal. 5:22-25, Js.3:17-18). The greatest of them is Godly love. (1 Cor. 13:11-13). This is not to be confused with the counterfeit "love" of the world but is the true sacrificial love of God.

CHAPTER 7 - PITFALLS TO A LIFE OF FAITH

GOD'S ESTABLISHED ORDER - Ephesians 5:15 - 6:9

God established an order to everything in the universe, in the solar system, in nature, in mankind, in society and the family. When he created, he did not leave things to run their own course but ordained a disciplined orderly way for all things to function.

It is no good putting on God's armour if we are not keeping his order and the scriptures immediately before those on God's armour are to do with God's order: in society, in the home, in marriage, with children and in the workplace. They are repeated in Colossians 3:18-25 and they outline God's order and how it functions in mutual love and respect, not taking advantage of others but in humility and submission to one another. This order is not new but ancient and has endured for thousands of years. However, the "New Age Order" is attempting to overthrow this ancient order and change everything. (Dan.7:25).

When something is not working a sign is put up saying "out of order". Society is out of order and broken, resulting in ruined lives, rebellion and disrespect. God's order has been broken and we are suffering because of it. It is in this context that we are told to put on the armour of God and to stand against the devil's wiles. Soldiers must be disciplined, and part of our discipleship is to keep the order.

This is an important subject and requires sober consideration as to the reasons why things are so out of order with the sad result of broken marriages, broken lives and broken hearts. The devil knows the best way to cause problems is to destroy God's order. He works through "principalities and rulers of darkness" and millions of demons that cause disorder. In current times immoral things or not necessarily illegal and illegal things are not necessarily immoral. We all know people whose lives have been destroyed through the disorder of today.

If you pause and consider this you will get understanding why the world is in such a mess.

LACK OF FORGIVENESS   *Joseph, Job*

Forgiveness is an essential principle for everyone. It is impossible to go through life and not be hurt in some way. One of the greatest pitfalls in life is unforgiveness. Many of us find that to forgive is the hardest thing to do and we can end up becoming resentful, bitter and even hateful for real or imaginary reasons.

We need to forgive and be forgiven and forgiveness is central in the teaching of the Lord. He taught the disciples how to pray and this included the need to forgive and be forgiven. (Matt. 6:12). In his teaching he emphasized forgiveness and gave an important principle: we are forgiven to the extent we ourselves forgive others. (Matt. 6:14,15). In order to emphasize the importance of forgiveness Jesus told what seems, on face value, to be a very harsh parable. (Matt. 18:21-35). The lesson is that if we don't forgive those who sin against us then we ourselves will *not* be forgiven. We must decide.

To forgive, no matter how hard, is not an option but a command. (Col. 3:12,13). To forgive does not depend on an apology from the offender or restitution on their part but must come from the heart of the offended person. Unforgiveness does great harm to ourselves but forgiveness releases peace and mercy into both us and the situation and can bring healing to both sides of an altercation, dispute or something more serious. To forgive is therefore necessary for our own wellbeing.

When Jesus hung on the cross his very first cry was to forgive. It was also the cry of Stephen as he was stoned to death. I believe it was this cry that touched the heart of Saul who was watching, and turned him into a saint. (Acts 7:58-60). There is a law of God called the "Royal Law of Liberty". (James 1:25-27, 2:1-13). This law does not seek vengeance but shows mercy, even to one's enemies. (Rom. 12:17-21).

HOW TO HANDLE HURTS AND ATTACKS

We are encouraged to bring our hurts to God in prayer. If we do so in an attitude of forgiveness and obedience to the Lord, we are set free from resentment and bitterness and released from the hurt. We can in gratitude to him forgive others because he forgave us. Forgiveness is necessary for us more than for those who have caused us hurt. People who do not forgive end up in a dreadful state of bondage and can suffer psychologically and mentally, as well as having serious physical ailments. Demonic bondage can also come because of it. So, it is important for our own good, to genuinely forgive those who have hurt us. This releases us and brings them to a place where God can speak to them and help them.

If you are under spiritual attack, forgiveness is part of your victory. Take the breastplate of righteousness and the shield of faith and "cast your burden on the Lord and he will sustain you: he will never permit the righteous to be moved". Encourage yourself in the promises of God's Word and enter his presence, receive forgiveness, love and healing. (Ps. 91, Ps. 55:22, Matt. 11:28-30, John 10:28,29).

THE PRINCIPLE OF CONFESSION AND CLEANSING

Believers are not perfect and can at times fall. This is because although we have been justified, we are not yet glorified. So, what should we do when we fail, make mistakes, and even fall in sin?

We are told what to do - to confess, <u>not to a priest but to the Lord himself</u> who is both *faithful* and *just* to *forgive* us and *cleanse* us from *all* unrighteousness. (1 Jn. 1:3-10). Some believers find it difficult to believe that the Lord will immediately forgive them once they have confessed but that is what he does. He does not hold it against us in some kind of grievance or as a means to manipulate us. The devil is very cunning in making God's children feel condemned when they are not. Satan brings us into condemnation but scripture says that we are not condemned. (Rom. 8:33,34). If you suffer from condemnation then it is the work of the enemy, not the Holy Spirit who works in our hearts to bring *conviction,* which is different from *condemnation*: conviction leads to confession, cleansing and forgiveness.

Do you have to confess to a priest? The answer is no, we are not forgiven through proxy, Jesus alone forgives us. There may, however, be a need if you have wronged a person to go to that person and confess your fault to them and if necessary them to you. (Js. 5:16, Matt. 5:23-26, 18:15, Gal. 6:1,2). I would offer a word of caution here and say that one must be very careful about confessing sins to just anyone. It can cause untold damage if that person cannot be trusted to keep confidences. Neither are we permitted to share another person's faults with anyone else unless we have been given approval to do so. It is a matter of honour before the Lord, who judges the hearts of all men, and severe repercussions can come upon those who do not maintain godly integrity. (Pr. 16:2).

WALKING IN THE LIGHT

Once we acknowledge our need of cleansing from sin and accept correction from the Lord, he is *faithful* and *just* to *forgive* us and *cleanse* us from *all* unrighteousness. (1 Jn. 1:9).

This principle is illustrated by the way the Lord, on the last night of his earthly life, washed the feet of the disciples. (Jn. 13:3-10). This was normally the task of a servant. People in those times walked everywhere and their feet became dirty and needed washing. Peter did not understand what Jesus did and protested, saying he needed his whole body washed, but Jesus said only his feet needed washing because he was already clean. What Jesus did was symbolic of our need to be washed as we walk in a world that rubs dirt off on us. We need daily cleansing and this comes from regular reading of the Word and when necessary, confession. God's Word has a cleansing affect upon us. (Eph. 5:26). Notice how John makes a difference between walking in darkness and walking in light. Because believers walk in light and are in fellowship with both the Father and the Son they are cleansed from *all* sin by the blood of Jesus Christ. (1 Jn. 1:3,7). If we trip up and fall, our fellowship is not broken because we walk in the light and our confession immediately maintains it. This is possible because Jesus is our advocate with the Father and defends us. (1 Jn. 2:1,2). He is our propitiation and "atoning sacrifice". There is a "putting off putting on" principle likened to the Old Testament practice of confession to the priests followed by sacrificial cleansing. The difference is that we don't go to an earthly priest or bring sacrifices but to our High Priest and his shed blood. (Heb. 7:24-27).

The Lord said to his people that he would not remember their sins. (Isa. 43:25, Ps. 103:12). If he has forgotten them, who are we to remember them? We must of course learn from them but God entirely eradicates them. The apostle Paul wrote that he had not reached perfection but, "forgetting those things that are past", he pressed on to the calling of God. (Phil. 3:12-15 NLB).

Confession is the principle we must practice in a life of faith: daily confession when it is necessary, putting off sin and putting on forgiveness. When you received Christ, you were buried with him and died to sin. Your sins are dead and buried and you have now been given Christ's righteousness. If your sins are buried then they must remain buried: don't go back and dig them up like old bones. Walk in his forgiveness and when necessary cast every sin into the grave of forgiveness and forgetfulness.

THE PRINCIPLE OF SOWING

There is a well-known saying: "What goes round, comes round". Jesus taught this in relation to spiritual things, one of which is hasty judgment of others. (Matt. 7:1-5). We are told not to judge hypocritically or self-righteously. At the same we must be wary of "dogs" (v 6, people of untrustworthy character), false prophets (v 15), and of those who have no "fruit" in their lives (v16). We are instructed to test false spirits and judge all things, but not condemn those who, like ourselves, are weak and subject to failure. This instruction is a warning not to make hasty condemnatory judgments of others. We must not allow a critical attitude to control us. Harsh judgment of others will boomerang back on us.

There is another saying, "What you sow you reap". This too is a scriptural principle. (Gal. 6:7-10). It is a natural, financial and spiritual law. God loves a cheerful generous giver. (2 Cor. 9:5-14). The Lord expects us to be good stewards of all he has given us, whether natural or supernatural. We must be faithful in all things. This principle is true in financial matters. If you honour the Lord, he will honour you. The reward in giving is very real. (Prov. 3:9). There is another saying: "It is more blessed to give than to receive". (Acts 20:35). We cannot buy spiritual wealth but God rewards true giving, not necessarily in monetary ways but in spiritual ways.

Sadly, in recent years there have been "prosperity preachers" who have taken this teaching completely out of context, thereby taking advantage of God's people and cajoling them to give to their own private funds. These people have thereby consequently become very wealthy. Their method is to use scripture to mislead people into giving money to them with the belief that if they do, they themselves will get a huge amount back. There are now multimillion-dollar preachers who have personally benefitted, while much of the world is suffering. I don't believe this is what God intended. It is one thing to give to God's work but another to give to unscrupulous people who get rich. Jesus spoke about the deception of wealth and there are many warnings in scripture that people who fall into the trap of greed and covetousness will themselves be enslaved. (Matt. 13:22, Mk. 4:18,19, 10:23-25, 1 Tim. 3:3,8, Jude 11, 2 Pet. 2:15). Preachers who do this must repent or they will face consequences before the Lord. Sadly, through the centuries the church has at times become excessively rich and built glorious buildings and accumulated much wealth. However, all the riches of this present age will come to nothing. (Rev.18:11-17).

Jesus has a message to the very rich and that is to give it away, and he has a message to those that are poor and have nothing and that is to trust him for a great reward. (Lk. 4:24,18:18-23, Js. 5:1-, Lk. 21:1-4). God has great rewards in heaven for all who are faithful to him. (Lk.14:12-14). He generously rewards those who give with a pure heart. We are instructed to care for our parents, older people, widows and orphans, the destitute, and all in need. (Eph.6:1-3, 1 Tim. 5:1-3). Every believer needs to develop avenues of giving, whether to the poor and needy, or people they know and love, or to genuine Gospel work.

CHAPTER 8 - KEYS TO GROWING IN CHRIST

The way to grow in a life of faith is to <u>read</u> the Bible, <u>pray</u>, have <u>fellowship</u> and <u>attend</u> a "body of believers" that provides sound teaching. By doing these four things you put yourself in the best possible place to grow and receive guidance, encouragement and support. (Heb. 10:23-25). They are keys whereby your faith can grow. The first believers were devoted to them and grew in faith. (Acts 2:41-47). One important thing is to partake of Breaking of Bread, also called Communion or the "Lord's Supper". It is best done collectively with others and we do it in remembrance of the Lord's death. (1 Cor. 11:20-26). It is a "spiritual meal" based on the Passover and the bread should be unleavened and the grape juice should be non-alcoholic (to not place temptation before others). (1 Cor. 5:7,8, Deut.16:2,3). They are emblems and do not carry some kind of power as thought in the practice of "last rights". Nevertheless, they are important in that the juice of the grape represents Christ's blood shed for the remission of sin, and unleavened bread represents his sinless body. Leaven is a symbol of sin and should *not* be used in Communion as it totally violates the meaning. Some churches use leavened bread but it is a tradition that compromises the symbolic truth of God's Word. Neither can communion cleanse us from sin. It is not wine that cleanses us but the blood of Christ which it represents. (1 Jn.1:7).

THE LAW OF DOUBT AND THE LAW OF FAITH

There are two conflicting laws that influence almost everyone – the law of faith and the law of doubt. In the Bible doubt is called unbelief. (Js. 1:6-8, 4:8). The law of doubt hinders, restricts and blocks our ability to function properly and grow as children of God. God always blesses and responds to faith not doubt, and we are to build up our faith. <u>It might surprise you to know that one of the keys to building our faith is trouble and adversity</u>. When things go wrong, we often react by asking, "Why did this happen to me?" The answer may well be "to build your faith". (1 Pet.1:3-9).

<u>Jesus encouraged</u> people to have faith and he did things to build up

and strengthen their faith. He told his disciples to do things, such as pray for the sick. (Matt. 10:8, 14:16). Sometimes he allowed things to happen in order to stretch their faith. One such time was when he sent the disciples ahead of him to cross the lake of Galilee while he stayed behind. The disciples were alone when a violent storm hit them. After a while Jesus appeared walking on the water and he made as if he would go right past them. When Peter cried out, "If it is you Lord, tell me to come to you", Jesus commanded him to come, and when he began to sink Jesus lifted him up and said, "You of little faith, why did you doubt?" (Matt. 24:31).

Another instance was when he told the blind man to go to the pool of Siloam and wash. (Jn. 9:6,7). This blind man had to negotiate a difficult obstacle course to get there but this was to build his faith up to receive healing. Faith will be tested and we should expect this and allow trials to strengthen our faith. We must build our faith and not give in to doubts. This was illustrated by the man who battled with doubt but nevertheless was honest enough to confess it to Jesus. (Mk. 9:24). The Lord did not condemn him when he asked for help to overcome his unbelief. We have to face our doubts, confess them and overcome them. The apostle James wrote that our faith will be tested, and warned us not to give in to doubt, because doubt cannot receive the promises of God nor be guided by his wisdom. (Js. 1:2-8, 4:8). Doubt produces sin, and faith produces perseverance, and we should look beyond the trial to what can come from it.

A life of faith achieves impossible things. The lives of many great men and women testify of their faith. Hebrews chapter 11 is called "the faith chapter" and records some of the great Biblical "heroes of faith": how they overcame massive obstacles, won victories over huge armies, faced wild animals, even triumphed over death itself. The Bible says "With God nothing is impossible". Outside of God's love there is nothing greater than to have faith in God: love and faith together are the strongest powers God makes available to man.

You might like to make a study of each life mentioned in this chapter and discover more about the lives of these men and women.

GOD'S WORD - THE BIBLE

One of the most important keys to spiritual growth is reading the Bible. "As newborn babes desire the pure milk of the word that you may grow thereby". (1 Pet. 2:1-3). This scripture mentions two vital keys: one is to trust the Lord like children trust their Father and the other is to grow by reading the Bible.

Jesus said that unless we are converted and become as little children, we cannot enter the Kingdom of God. (Matt. 18:2-5, Luke 18:16,17). As little children we have to start again and learn new things and unlearn old things. As babies desire milk, so we are to desire the "milk of the word": in other words, to start with basic Bible teaching that is easy to understand and then mature on deeper things. We have already considered the basic principles of Christ's teaching but we need to feed on the written Word more and more. I encourage believers to read the Gospels again and again until familiar with them. They are the story of Jesus. The first three Gospels are very similar whereas the fourth records other events and spiritual truths.

The Bible is in two parts, the Old and New Testaments. The Old is the account of God's revelation to man through history up to the time of the great prophets before Jesus was born. The New Testament is the unique account of the birth, life, death and resurrection of Jesus, as foretold in the Old, and the subsequent coming of the Holy Spirit bringing salvation to all people, starting in Jerusalem and extending to all quarters of the known world. (Lk. 24:25-27).

Christians believe that the Bible is inspired by God and is true and authoritative. There has always been attacks against the Bible by those who do not believe it but through 2000 years it has withstood every attack and is acknowledged today as the most published and read book in the world. It has stood the test of time.

THE BIBLE IS THE "CANON OF SCRIPTURE"

Jesus believed the Old Testament, and said that his own words would not pass away. (Matt. 24:35). The apostle Paul wrote that Biblical Scriptures are inspired by God and point us to salvation through faith in Christ. (2 Tim. 3:14-17). The Bible is the most attacked book, yet many great men and women through history believed it. Jesus himself believed the historicity, authenticity, preservation and accuracy of the Old Testament. He believed in Adam and Eve, the Flood, Jonah and every other statement in it. The New Testament tells us about Jesus and it was written by people who knew him intimately before and after his resurrection. (1 Jn.1:1-5).

Our modern Bible is translated from many ancient texts and there is more proof of its authenticity than for any other book in history. Most modern translations enhance and complement each other but a few are considered dubious. Some Bibles have study notes included in them which can be helpful but a word of warning must be sounded: be very careful of some of the doctrines found in these notes, they are not authoritative and just because they are in it doesn't mean they are true.

There is no substitute for reading the Bible and it is a priority for every believer for their life of faith.

KEYS TO READING THE BIBLE

One of the <u>key</u> principles needed to understand the Bible is "to keep the context" when we read it. This is a basic <u>rule of interpretation</u> which must be strictly adhered to when reading any document in any language. This rule observes the portions that precede or follow a passage or word and thereby establish its meaning. Nothing should be taken "out of context" to the main subject matter. The historical and cultural context must also be maintained.

There are different approaches to reading the Bible. One is to read the Bible from beginning to end but I encourage new believers to start with the New Testament. When familiar with it, then begin to discover the Old Testament but continue in the New as well. I also suggest that one tries to read a book at a time, not necessarily all in one go but to read it as a whole. In this way one gets an overall understanding of it.

Having once read one portion it does not lose its value and the more often it is read the more truth it will yield. Get a notepad and write down things the Lord shows you. The Bible has different "levels" and there are places you will find easier to understand than others. God "speaks" through it so expect him to speak to you. You will find at times a verse will "come alive" and jump out at you and you get insight you have not had before. It is a "living Word".

Obtain a good translation that you find easy to read and get into a routine of reading every day. Try and ensure you will not be disturbed while you read. Switch off the TV and pray before you read, asking the Lord to help you understand. Read slowly and talk to the Lord as you do. Allow the Lord to talk to you through his Spirit and learn to listen to him in your spirit. Make it a sharing time with the Lord. He will be with you and it will become a time of meeting with him. As a result, you will be able to receive spiritual sustenance firsthand from the Lord instead of secondhand from someone else. The Lord gave daily Manna (bread from heaven) to the Children of Israel to feed on. (Jn. 6:31-58). It was fresh every day and never old or stale but they themselves had to collect it. The Bible is like heavenly Manna

Praying is talking to the Lord and having had a time of Bible reading and praying you can continue the rest of the day walking with the Lord. Throughout the day you can talk to him wherever you are, at work or school and wherever you go, praying in every situation.

HOW TO DO A BIBLE STUDY FOR YOURSELF

It is very rewarding to develop your Bible reading into actual studies on a particular subject of interest. Many Bibles have textual references which link scriptures of the same theme. They form a chain from one scripture to another and thereby expand the meaning and depth of the original scripture.

Get yourself a Bible Concordance which will enable you to look up words. Some concordances give the meaning of the original Hebrew or Greek languages. Keep a <u>journal</u> of your discoveries and write down all the things that come to your mind in your daily reading with the Lord. Put a date on it so you can refer to it later, especially if you feel there is something important the Lord has said to you. Choose a topic such as faith, or another of importance, and begin. You will be amazed at what you can discover and what God will show you.

PRAYER

A very important key to personal growth is private prayer. Jesus said *"Go into your room and when you have shut the door pray to your Father who is in the "secret place" and your Father who sees in secret will reward you openly"*. (Matt. 6:5-8).

We have looked at prayer in the context of our daily quite time with God but there is the need to expand our prayers to pray specifically for special needs or circumstances. There were times when Jesus withdrew from others and spent time in prayer, and there will be times for you too when you should pray for special needs of your own and of others. There are also times when you may be prompted to fast. (Matt. 6:16-18, Acts 13:2,3). Ask a mature believer about this.

Our every need should be brought to God in prayer. The prayer of faith is one of the most powerful keys God has given us. It is so powerful that it opens and closes things in heaven and on earth. (Matt. 16:19). Elijah is an example of prayer. (Js. 5:17,18).

KEYS TO PRAYING – THE LORD'S PRAYER

Praying is a key in a believer's life: praying alone and with others, praying in the Spirit, praying in trouble, praying for protection, praying for guidance, praying for provision, praying for the nation – there is nothing we cannot pray for. There is a lovely old hymn about prayer: –
"What a friend we have in Jesus, All our sins and griefs to bear, What a privilege to carry, Everything to him in prayer, Oh what peace we often forfeit, Oh what needless pain we bear, All because we do not carry, Everything to him in prayer".

The Lord Jesus gave instructions on how to pray and outlined a model for prayer with its most important aspects. (Matt. 6:7-15). I don't believe that he meant this prayer to be said by rote but if one prays its content, with faith and conviction, it is very meaningful. The opening part of this prayer is to establish to whom we are praying; it is to "our heavenly <u>Father</u>". We have already considered the necessity of knowing God as our Father through Jesus Christ. It is in his name that we approach God. His name is holy, to be venerated and consecrated and greatly revered. It is not a flippant thing to call God our Heavenly Father and to use the name of the Most High God in prayer.

The next thing he said is, "Your <u>Kingdom come, your will be done</u>". This infers that we should have some knowledge of what God's will is. We do not have the prerogative to pray our own will. This is a great *principle* in prayer: we are praying for his will, not our own. (Mk.14:36). Before we can ask for something, we must have a conviction that it is God's will. This requires diligence on our part to discover what the will of God is, from scripture, in counsel with others or by waiting on the Lord. Once we have a conviction about what to pray, we can ask in full assurance and faith, confidently knowing that what we ask for we will receive.

Next, our prayers include our daily needs: our "<u>daily bread</u>". I would discourage people to come to God with a long "shopping list" of what they want, but there are times when we all have needs. George Muller pioneered children's homes in Britain and there were times when he did not know from where the next mouthful of food was coming. He prayed and the Lord always miraculously provided. God is able to provide our daily needs but people can be confused sometimes as to what is needed and what is merely wanted.

The next part is crucial in all our prayers, "<u>forgive us our trespasses, even as we forgive those that sin against us</u>". We have already looked at the process of forgiveness and it should be done on a daily basis if necessary. We cannot come to God in prayer and think he will answer if we are holding on to unforgiveness.

Next, we pray for being led "out of temptation, (testing and trial) and for deliverance from evil". We all have trials and temptations, and God is willing and able to deliver us from them. We should also pray for and live in his protection. In fact, we should be mindful all the time of this for we live in a wicked age and need to stay in God's protection. We must learn to listen to the Spirit of God and hear when he warns us about danger. Many scriptures speak of keeping close to the Lord and of hiding in the secret place of the Most High God. (Ps. 27:11,12, 32:7, 46:1 91). The prayer ends with, "For yours is the kingdom, the power and the glory". This is praise, affirmation and worship of God.

PRAISE AND THANKSGIVING

Praise and thanksgiving is a key to a life of faith. They should be regular expressions in our prayers. Praise is a vital part of achieving victory in a test. In the Old Testament we read how God's people prevailed in difficult circumstances when they praised him. (2 Chr. 20:15-23). Many of the Psalms are songs of praise. (Ps. 67, 148, 150). When Paul and Silas had been beaten badly and thrown in prison, instead of complaining they sang praises and the Lord delivered them with a mighty earthquake. (Acts 16:25,26).

Praise is called the "sacrifice of praise" and sometimes it might be hard to do, but it pleases God and is worth the "effort", for it brings joy and gives victory. Praise is a key principle for every believer. Psalm 100:4 says we are to "enter His gates with thanksgiving and His courts with praise". As you develop praise and thanksgiving you will find it easy to come into his Presence for it breaks the invisible fetters that often bind us. Praise and thanksgiving, empowers our prayers.

PRAYING IN THE SPIRIT

Praying in the Spirit is a vital key for life in the Spirit. Prayer is not meant to be repetitive or done in rote but spontaneous and prompted by the Holy Spirit. In your prayers you can be led by God in praying and singing in the Spirit. The apostle Paul also spoke of the ability to speak in unknown "tongues". (1 Cor. 14:14,15). This is a gift that the

Lord gives believers for their personal edification to help them pray more effectively. (1 Cor. 14:2-5). It is when the Holy Spirit takes over and prays through us, expressing the perfect mind of God in a language unknown to us. (Rom. 8:26,27). Praying in the Spirit is not limited to praying in "tongues" but is when the Holy Spirit creates, directs and empowers our prayers. It is a dimension of prayer in which he is in complete control. When one prays in the Spirit it is powerful, edifying and uplifting. Jude 20 - "beloved, building yourself up in your most holy faith, praying in the Holy Spirit".

Prayer is not confined to a church building but can be done anywhere, at any time, and in any situation. In your private prayers, you can pray out aloud and should do so regularly. You can also pray silently when no words cross you lips but are in your heart. You can pray anywhere, even in public silently. There will be times when you can only sigh or groan or weep when you pray. (Rom. 8:26,27). Corporate prayer is when believers pray together and is very powerful if done in agreement and one accord. (Acts 1:14, 4:24, 12:5,12, Matt. 18:19,20).

GIFTS FOR SPIRITUAL GROWTH - Eph. 4:11-16

Another key which the Lord provides for our growth is the ministry he places in his church. By attending a fellowship that functions with "ministry gifts" you will benefit from the maturity and loving care of others. God has given spiritual gifts to the corporate "body of Christ" in those who function as pastors, teachers, evangelists, prophets and apostles. (1 Cor. 12:28-31, Eph. 4:11-16). They complement each other and provide a balanced presentation of Biblical truth. These are "servant gifts", not for control but for serving. Sadly, they all too often have become "celebrity gifts" used for personal gain. Some believers follow these people instead of Jesus. Thousands of people follow so called "prophets" and "apostles" on social media or in large meetings and too often depend on their latest prophetic words or newest teaching instead of seeking Jesus and waiting upon him. (Matt. 17:4,5, 1 Cor.1:10-13, 3:4). This has birthed many cults. We are to follow Jesus not men. The true role of leaders is to ground and mature believers to rely on Jesus and, if necessary, to stand with him alone.

GIFTS OF THE HOLY SPIRIT – <u>1 Cor. 12:4-11</u>

God uses "gifts of his Spirit" to give comfort, encouragement and edification to believers. These gifts are listed as wisdom, knowledge, faith, healing, miracles, prophecy, discernment, tongues and interpretation. I believe these gifts still function and during fifty years of ministry have seen God work through them. Sadly, many churches don't believe they are valid or allow them. There is a great need to use these gifts in the correct way and they can be misused and abused due to lack of knowledge and sound teaching. The apostle Paul wrote, "Brothers and sisters, don't be children in your understanding of these things. Be innocent as babes when it comes to evil, but be mature in understanding matters of this kind". (1 Cor. 14:20 NLT).

GIFTS FOR GUIDANCE – John 16:3

The Lord also uses various ways to counsel and guide us. As already mentioned, one is through regular Bible teaching. This is the most important way to receive guidance. The Holy Spirit leads us into truth through the scriptures which are able to make us wise in all things pertaining to salvation. (Jn. 16:13). There are other ways, such as visions, prophecies and words of knowledge, but they must be handled correctly. The Holy Spirit is able to give divine knowledge to assist us especially in counselling, but one must be very careful before one reveals things about anyone that are personal. I am against the public disclosure of anyone's privacy without their consent. It is wise to seek counsel from mature believers and it seldom comes through just one way. (2 Cor. 13:1).

Be especially careful of those who say they have "a direct word from the Lord for you" whether in private or public gatherings. People have been misled by utterances purporting to be direct from God. We all can receive counsel but we need to judge any words given in God's name. Some people speak today as if the Lord himself is speaking through them and they put themselves in the category of Old Testament prophets who spoke words coming direct from God himself. These words were written down and became part of scripture.

Today, however, the "canon of scripture must have nothing added or taken away. (Rev. 22:18,19). We need to respect God's Word and not confuse his Word with our words which, by writing down and circulating messages as if God is speaking in the first-person tense, this modern-day practice is prone to do. (Ezk.13:6-10). Speaking for God in a direct manner is *not* sound New Testament practice. In the Old Testament God spoke *directly* and God still does today when he speaks personally through his Spirit to someone: he uses the "direct tense". (Acts 9:15, 10:20, 13:2, 18:10). If, however, a prophetic word is given to the corporate body of Christ it should be given in an indirect manner; it is not the direct words of God but a person speaking their own words, hopefully under the inspiration of the Spirit. (Luke 1:46, 67). The practice of speaking as if God is speaking, although widespread today, was *not* done in the early church or by early Pentecostals, but has crept in through the "Charismatic Movement". It is "new age" prophesying, a practice, albeit dressed up in Christian terms, which elevates man into assumed divinity. It has produced confusion and false doctrines. Every prophetic utterance must be judged and is not automatically from God. (1 Jn. 4:1, 1 Cor. 14:29). When Paul was on his way to Rome, he was told several times that suffering would befall him but he was not deterred and pressed on. (Acts 20:22,23, 21:4,11). Although the Holy Spirit spoke, nowhere did anyone say "thus says the Lord" or considered it a binding instruction.

To benefit from prophetic gifts, it is wise to use the indirect tense. For more on this I would direct the earnest believer to the classic book by Harold Horton, "The Gifts of the Spirit", in which he explains this principle: *"It is not the Lord who speaks, but the prophet:"*. None of those filled with the Spirit on the day of Pentecost spoke *for* God but *about* God. (Acts 2:11). Horton explains that one should not speak, *"I the Lord will hear you"*, but *"The Lord hear you"*. (See books in Reference Notes - p 98.)

THE PEACE OF GOD IS THE KEY TO EVERY SITUATION

This is one of the greatest keys to knowing God's guidance. When we are walking in the will of God, we have peace; when we are out of step or going the wrong way, we will not have peace. Peace is a way that God confirms his will in our lives. We can at times be in a great storm of adversity and yet be filled with peace. If you have made a decision, or are doing something yet have no peace, then you need to pause and ask the Lord why. If you have no peace, then you may need to seek new direction. (Phil. 4:6-10). Sometimes we don't understand why we have no peace, but the peace God gives transcends our minds and leads us in ways we may not comprehend. It is like an umpire which overrules all else and leads us in God's way.

KEYS TO WITNESSING

The Lord instructed his disciples to share the Gospel with others whenever there are opportunities to do so. (Matt. 28:19, Mk. 16:15, Matt. 22:9,10). This is not necessarily preaching at them but sharing with them when possible. We are not told to convert people; we are told to witness to them about Christ. There are several ways in which we can witness. One is through our own testimony. This is an excellent way to share what Christ has done for us and because it is personal it carries enormous impact, especially if others see in us a life of faith. The greatest witness, that does not even need words, is the witness of a changed life.

It is also done by sowing seeds of love, gentleness and kindness. People respond to the fruit of the Spirit of God. It is not just our words but our lives that count. The fruit of God's Love is the most powerful fruit to sow in someone's life. (1 Cor. 3:1-3, 13:1-13). Seed is found in fruit and when the fruit is eaten so the seed is too. It then lodges in people's hearts and bears fruit, sometimes years later. We cannot force people to believe; we can only tell them about the Lord and the rest is up to them. If we are sharing the fruits of his Spirit then the Lord will water the seeds we plant and bring them to life.

Another way to witness is to use scripture to create interest and impart truth. This is what Philip did when he spoke to a man who asked him what a certain scripture meant. (Acts 8:30-35). Yet another way is to pray for someone. If a person is sick, afraid or in sorrow they will often accept a short prayer. Ask them first and if they agree then pray with respect, compassion and faith. God will use you to touch their hearts.

Finally, witnessing is not necessarily preaching a sermon or trying to explain the whole Bible at one time. It can be just a word at a time. "God Bless You" are three of the most powerful words we can say. They can change a heart. If we sow good seed through a good life then God will water it, even if it lies dormant for years. God's Word is living and comes alive when he waters it. We will never know how we have impacted others until we stand before the Lord.

KEYS TO LEAD SOMEONE TO CHRIST

It is a privilege to help someone to receive Christ as Lord and Saviour. You do not have to be an ordained minister or have a degree in theology to do this. If you know Christ as Lord you are able to help others to know him too. Neither do you have to use a lot of scriptures, sometimes the less the better. By quoting too many it can become confusing. However, scripture *must* be used to establish a decision and make it valid. People are not converted by our own convictions but through faith in God and his Word. (1 Pet. 1:23). Salvation is based on the incorruptible and enduring word of God. God gives his Word and we believe it.

Some key scriptures to help someone receive Jesus as Lord.

All people have fallen short of God's standards. (Rom. 3:21-23-26).
No one is righteous. (Rom. 3:10).
God gives us eternal life through Jesus Christ. (John 3:16,17).
If we believe and receive Jesus we are born again and become God's children. (John 1:12-13).
Whoever confesses Jesus as Lord and calls on him will be saved. (Rom. 10:9,10,13).

CHAPTER 9 – PROMISES FOR OUR FUTURE

God has given us many great promises for the future he has planned for us. (1 Pet.1:1-13). He is making a new "heaven and earth" and one day heaven will come down to earth and the whole of creation will be perfect. (Rev.21;1-5). We will have an eternal home in a city called "New Jerusalem" where there is no death, sorrow, pain or crying. (Rev.21:4). There are so many scriptures declaring the certainty of God's promises that to doubt them is simply unbelief.

HEAVEN IS OUR HOME

Although the Kingdom of God cannot yet be seen it nevertheless exists and will fully come when Jesus comes. He is even now preparing a heavenly home for us in his Father's house. (Jn. 14:1-4). When Jesus spoke of heaven, he could have described streets of gold, angels and all the splendour, but he did not, he described it as his house. We must never forget that this present world is not our home and we are pilgrims passing through. (Heb. 11:10, 12:22, 13:14, Rev. 21:1-4). We are promised a wonderful home where we will live in peace and safety forever. Nothing can hurt us there, no thief can break in, and there is no decay. It is a place of joy, peace, security, purity and absolute perfection. It is impossible to fully describe it. (Matt. 5:12, 1 Cor.2:9).

<u>We are heirs of God's Kingdom</u> - (Rom. 8:16-18, Gal. 4:7 Js.2:5). Nothing we experience on earth can compare to the rewards we will have in heaven. No matter how much one has suffered, the reward in heaven will be so great that it is beyond our ability to grasp. Whatever is done for Christ will be rewarded. Rewards are not earned but given. (Heb. 11:6). The greatest reward is to be an heir of Christ and a son or daughter of God. He is our hope of glory and we are heirs of all God's riches. (Col. 1:27, Phil. 4:19).

THE KEY TO A LIFE OF FAITH IS <u>HOPE</u>

There is a wonderful and great promise to which we must hold firm in faith: it is the <u>"Blessed Hope" of the return of Jesus.</u> (Jn. 14:3,4, Titus

2:11-13). Jesus gave a promise to every believer that he will come again and receive them to himself. It is this promise that gives us security and hope in a world that has nothing permanent to offer. Jesus said, "**_Seek first the Kingdom of God and His righteousness and all these things shall be added to you._**" (Matt. 6:33). How we live now will determine our rewards in the coming Kingdom.

This is the hope to which we must hold fast. (Heb.3:6, 4:14-16). We are not to be moved away from the *full assurance of hope* that is set before us. (Heb. 6:11-19). It is this sure and steadfast hope that anchors our soul and reaches right into the throne room of heaven and we can enter there to receive mercy and grace whenever we need help. There is a hymn –

"We have an anchor that keeps the soul, Steadfast and sure as the billows roll, Fastened to the Rock that cannot move, Grounded firm and deep in the Saviour's love."

"So do not throw away your confidence, it will be greatly rewarded. You need to persevere, so that when you have done the will of God, you will receive what he has promised. For in just a very little while, He who is coming will come and not delay."
(Heb. 10:35,36 NIV).

There are different views as to how Christ will come but the important thing is to believe he will return. He is our "blessed hope" in a world that has no hope. It is this that makes us never give up and ensures our salvation. (Rom. 8:24, 1 Thess. 5:1-8).

Hope is the Key that keeps our hearts and minds. It is not an uncertain hope as the world has, but a hope that is so sure and steadfast that it can never be moved and is an anchor that keeps us through the storms of life. Faith, hope and love abide forever. (1 Cor.13:13).

The one great key to living a life of faith is to never turn back.
There is a beautiful song which expresses this –

I have decided to follow Jesus, x3
No turning back, no turning back.
The world behind me the cross before me, x3
No turning back, No turning back.

The last words of the apostle Peter were, **"Therefore, brethren, be even more diligent to make your call and election sure, for if you do these things you will never stumble; for so an entrance will be supplied to you abundantly into the everlasting kingdom of our Lord and Saviour Jesus Christ** *(2 Pet. 1:10,11).* **Grow in the grace and knowledge of our Lord and Saviour Jesus Christ".** *(3:18).*

The psalmist said, **"One thing I have desired of the Lord, that will I seek; that I may dwell in the house of the Lord all the days of my life to behold the beauty of the Lord, and to inquire in His temple."** *(Psalm 27:4)*

....

YOUR PRAYER

Lord Jesus, I believe you are the eternal Son of God and that you died for my sins and rose again to give me eternal life.
I know I have sinned and I repent and confess all my sins to you and ask you to forgive me and cleanse me.
I receive you as my Lord and Saviour, and ask you to come into my life by your Spirit, and give me spiritual rebirth. I submit the rest of my life to you and believe I have now become a child of God.

....
.

If you have prayed this prayer then write your name here and start to grow in your faith as directed in this book. God bless you.

REFERENCE NOTES

Gifts of the Holy Spirit – the following books are helpful: "The Gifts of the Spirit", Harold Horton; "These Wonderful Gifts" – Michael Harper; "When the Spirit Speaks" – Warren D Bullock.

Creation – see Creation Ministries International, creation.com

The Resurrection
A famous American lawyer, Lewis Wallace (1827-1905) set out to write a book to disprove the resurrection of Christ. At the end of it he concluded, contrary to his predisposition, that Jesus Christ did indeed rise from the dead. He went on to write a book, "Ben Hur: A Tale of the Christ" which became an acclaimed film.
Another lawyer, from Britain, Frank Morison, who started as a skeptic affirmed the resurrection and wrote "Who Moved the Stone?"
The famous Harvard law professor Simon Greenleaf, considered to be the greatest authority on legal evidence, considered the evidence for the resurrection and was convinced that it was all historical fact.
Thomas Sherlock wrote, "The Trial of the Witnesses of the Resurrection of Jesus Christ" which placed the resurrection in a legally argued forum, and which was endorsed by the lawyer Irwin Linton and many others.
Ross Clifford wrote, "Leading Lawyer's Case for the Resurrection".

Judgment – "Hell" by Edward Fudge, a Reformed Theologian made a life-study of hell, judgment and eternity. See his other books.

....

Abbreviations used for Bible books:
Genesis – Gen. Exodus – Ex. Chronicles – Est.- Ester, Chr. Psalms – Ps. Isaiah – Isa. Mic. – Micah. Matthew – Matt. Mark – Mk. Luke – Lk. John – Jn. Romans – Rom. Corinthians – Cor. Ephesians – Eph. Philippians – Phil. Colossians – Col. Thessalonians – Thess. Timothy – Tim. Hebrews – Heb. James – Js. Peter – Pet. Revelation – Rev.

Bible translations used in this study are the New King James (NKJ), New International Version (NIV), New Living Translation (NLT), Amplified Bible (AB), Complete Jewish Bible (CJB).

ZECH 12:10
Zech 14 — Nuclear

8827324807 / 177049

Olive Spiritual = noble root is Abraham
Fig National
Vine Jesus
Commonwealth
Remnant.
GAL 6:16